What readers are saying about
Stroke Survivor:
A Story of Hope

"*Stroke Survivor: A Story of Hope* perfectly mixes creative coping techniques, respect for one another, and a dash of humor, as the writers provide a down-to-earth account of how they have chosen to deal with the toughest of circumstances. The honesty is refreshing, the insight is practical, and the transparency is touching. The 'real life' stuff that others might be afraid to verbalize helps me feel validated and more 'normal.'"

—Brenda Vert, wife of a spinal cord injury survivor;
former program director of Fresh Start,
a day program for survivors of brain injuries

"The Kvernens offer a touching and candid look at the real and often heart-wrenching journey of a stroke survivor and his wife, who together experience a sudden and overwhelming illness while in the prime of their lives. This book helps normalize the struggle for recovery for anyone affected by a life-changing disability, and it offers hope for emotional, relational, and spiritual healing in the midst of tragedy and trauma. A must-read for all who have been personally affected by devastating illness, as well as for professionals who provide care in a rehabilitation or long-term care setting."

—Ken Wadum, EdD, psychologist

"It is difficult to articulate what it is like to suddenly be thrust into the role of caregiver for a husband who has experienced brain injury. This book describes in detail some of those struggles and the adjustments that are needed when life with your loved one is turned upside down. In this story I found comfort in knowing I am not alone on this journey, as well as encouragement through reading the book's practical tips for coping."

—Sherrie Porterfield, wife of a brain injury survivor

"We work with traumatic brain injury survivors every day. They want hope and honest, practical information about how to handle their new circumstance. This inspiring story provides both."

—Kreg A. Kauffman, attorney

"This book could have been titled *Our Incredible Journey*, but the Kvernens have instead chosen to focus their message on helping others who face the challenges of a major stroke in the family. At the conclusion of each chapter, a practical list of 'What helped us cope and gave us hope' gives specific ideas of ways a family might want to reach out for the help they need. The authors' willingness to share strategies that were helpful to their family is a precious gift to others on this journey."

—Margaret Dahl, RN-BC,
nurse administrator, long-term care

"Historically, humans have supported each other through sharing stories. *Stroke Survivor: A Story of Hope* is a print version of this age-old concept of humans helping humans. With warmth, honesty, and humor, the author's impressive caregiving journey can help other caregivers alleviate guilt, accept challenges, and yes, find hope."

"This real life story truly informs and gives hope. Honest experiences and examples are shared with practical and concise ideas noted at the end of each chapter. The lists of 'What helped us cope and gave us hope' are deserving of their own publication. This twenty-year journey of the trials and triumphs of a stroke survivor and his family will inspire and encourage all those involved in the care of people with any disability. I would recommend this book to anyone who provides care for a stroke survivor."

"This book represents the emotional swings and struggles many people encounter after a stroke, including possible loss of life, rehabilitation, and life at home. Lots of information and helpful hints for survivors, families, and caregivers make this a must-read."

"With every chapter of *Stroke Survivor: A Story of Hope*, I was reminded of how recovery impacts each family member. I hope that anyone in this situation will find encouragement and hope through this book."

—Ann Petersen, MS, Vocational Rehabilitation,
sister of brain injury survivor

Stroke
Survivor

Stroke Survivor

A Story of Hope

Rosella & Don Kvernen

Two Harbors Press
212 3rd Avenue North, Suite 290
Minneapolis, MN 55401
612.455.2293
www.TwoHarborsPress.com

ISBN-13: 978-1-937928-08-7
LCCN: 2011943988

Distributed by Itasca Books

Book design by Wendy Arakawa
Cover photographs by Fagan Studios, Rochester, MN
Cover design by Panetta Design, Rochester, MN
Editor Marly Cornell
Printed in the United States of America

www.StrokeSurvivor-StoryofHope.com

To fellow stroke survivors and their families

Contents

Foreword

Standing beside my father-in-law's bed after his stroke, I often yearned for a book that would explain what we were living through, in non-medical terms. The medical staff tried to communicate with us, but there was a Grand Canyon-sized gap.

I finally asked for some written materials to help us understand. Pamphlets were dispensed, and we eagerly started reading. The materials were published using the same hard-to-comprehend language the medical personnel had been using. The family stacked them neatly in a corner until I finally tossed them.

We continued on as best we could, but the hopelessness started to pile up on our hearts. As I stood by Dad's bed, I thought about the book Rosella and Don were writing and wished I had a copy to read and give to my family members. Later, at Dad's funeral, I thought about Rosella and Don's book again. I'd met others in the hospital hallways who were also confused. I wanted this book for them—for the elderly woman who stood at her middle-aged son's bed and cried, not only over his circumstance but for her inability to comprehend it; and for the husband who roamed the halls, asking questions about his wife's hope of recovery, and returned to her room, still feeling like he just "couldn't get it." These families were told that their loved ones would recover, and they longed to know what that recovery might look like, or at least how others had handled the situation. One husband asked, "Is there a book with a recovery story in it we can read?" The staff had none to recommend. Neither did the pastor he asked next.

Families of stroke patients want more than medically correct terms—they need a real life story that informs and gives hope. *Stroke Survivor: A Story of Hope* is the book we have all wished for—a book that offers the reader courage in the midst of crisis. I am grateful for Rosella and Don's authenticity and transparency. Rosella's strength and Don's joy are contagious— diving into these pages will allow you to "catch" a little of both.

—Joy Dekok, author coach,
and someone who has lived through a loved one's stroke

Introduction

Daily, perhaps hourly, my husband is conscious of how a stroke radically changed his life. The stroke Don suffered in 1991...

- paralyzed his right side,
- significantly impaired his use and comprehension of words,
- destroyed his ability to read and write,
- gave him seizures,
- altered his relationships with family and friends,
- dashed his plans, and
- left him no longer able to work as a psychologist.

However, after two decades, the core of Don's former self remains. He is still the loving, gentle, funny, wise, and wonderful man he was before his stroke—most of the time. I am proud of Don, especially of his character and inner drive that helped him deal with the aftermath of his stroke in such a remarkable way. He inspires those of us who have walked with him through his struggles.

Don has not made a complete, miraculous comeback. For twenty years, he has persisted through disability and frustration, either to recover and improve or to compensate for what he cannot change. Don has made great strides in his recovery even though he often says, "I'm about a quart low."

This is not a technical how-to book for dealing with stroke but rather a true, personal story of persevering through adversity. Don's stroke devastated him, and it also diverted our sixteen-year-old-son, Jon, our twelve-year-old son, Josh, and me from an active and happy family and social life to a completely different and challenging reality.

We share our story to encourage those who cope with difficulties and hopelessness after a stroke. As we have dealt with the outcome and the severity of Don's stroke, we learned that, even if we cannot all return to the lives we used to live, we can hold onto the *most important* things in life. We can still experience joy and fulfillment; we can retain purpose and hope.

We write our story also for those within a stroke survivor's inner circle who are family members, care partners, or friends. Our sons and I survived Don's stroke and moved on to enjoy life again. You will survive, and you will hurt less over time; there is hope for you, too. May our story give you courage to carry on and insights that help you continue to love and understand your survivor.

Don has difficulty expressing himself; but when he urged me to write this book, he said in essence, "As a psychologist, I helped many people deal with tragedies and problems in their lives. After my stroke, I had to listen to my own advice. I want to share in our book what helped me survive. I also want to tell people about the teaching method that started me back toward reading when nothing else worked. Most of all, I want to give hope to fellow survivors and warn them not to believe anyone who tells them they will not improve if recovery does not come immediately. I still continue to improve."

Don's stroke left him with significant *aphasia*, which means he struggles with words, whether written, spoken, or heard. Although Don is unable to type and cannot write well enough to literally write this book, he provided the impetus; the result is a collaboration. Don wants me to tell the whole story, even those parts that are not pretty. Because Don cannot tell things exactly the way he thinks them in his mind, I have composed quotes for him with his approval and tell our story primarily from my perspective.

—Don's wife, Rosella

Chapter 1
Talking in Gibberish

"Hi, this is Amy at the office. Don had a strange spell a few minutes ago. He talked in gibberish for about five minutes. Ken and Don just left for the emergency room at St. Marys, and Don asked me to tell you to meet him there." (St. Marys Hospital is part of the Mayo Clinic in Rochester, Minnesota.)

"How is he right now?" I asked as my anxiety rose.

"When Don's client came out for help, Ken and I both went into Don's office and heard him talking quite strangely; but by the time he left, Don seemed normal again."

I hurried to the hospital, wondering what was happening. When I arrived at the ER, Don's vital signs were already being monitored. The doctors ordered blood work, an electrocardiogram, an echocardiogram, a CT scan, and an IV of heparin to inhibit the formation of clots. As a former nurse, I felt accustomed to an ER setting. I was not overly concerned because Don seemed normal when he answered questions and complied with frequent checks for neurological symptoms.

While we waited between tests, Don and I chatted. He said he felt bad that he must have scared his new client, and he expressed more concern about his secretary rescheduling the rest of his clients for the day than about his condition.

Later that afternoon while still in the ER, Don experienced

another episode of impaired speech. He sounded strange as he mixed up words and ideas, but he had no other abnormal physical symptoms.

I called our boys once they arrived home from school on the bus. Jon was a junior in high school and Josh a sixth grader in our small town west of Rochester. I explained to them why their dad was in the ER. Since Don was in the middle of his second episode, I decided I should stay with him, and the boys promised to start their homework. I called to update the boys during the afternoon. Don's second spell lasted about three hours. When it passed, the ER doctors decided to admit Don for observation on a neurology unit.

The hospital staff said the nurses on the new unit needed time to settle Don into his room, so I drove home. The boys and I grabbed a bite to eat, and we came back to the hospital. During the evening, Don again seemed normal. He joked and bantered with the hospital staff, a few visitors, and with our boys and me.

As we left, we hugged Don and I said, "I love you. See you tomorrow."

Don replied, "Call me in the morning to see when you should come to pick me up."

Don and I had a great life. We loved each other, and our two sons brought us great joy and pride. Don and I both volunteered with our kids' school, sports, and church activities. Don had found his calling in life as a counselor. I loved being a homemaker. My passion was to nurture my husband and sons, manage our household, and help people where I saw needs. We had wonderful friends, and our lives had purpose.

A busy sixteen-year-old, Jon carried a full academic load and dreamed of becoming a doctor. He played trombone in band and jazz band, sang in an ensemble, enjoyed his church youth activities, and ran the soundboard at church and school. He played baseball and liked to water-ski and downhill ski.

Josh, our twelve-year-old, also enjoyed school and played trombone like his brother. He attended kids' activities at church and sang in the children's choir I directed. Josh played baseball and collected baseball cards. He sometimes babysat, and he loved to play with his friends.

The morning after Don was hospitalized, I woke the boys to get ready for school. I remembered how busy patients and hospital staff were at the beginning of the day shift, so I ate breakfast with the boys and sent them out to the bus before I called Don. I was not particularly worried. I intended to skip my morning plans, bring Don home sometime before lunch, and take Jon to a meeting in the later afternoon.

After many rings, Don answered his phone. He spoke in profoundly slurred, incoherent words. During my short attempt at conversation, I quickly realized something was seriously wrong. The moment I said goodbye to Don, a vice-like feeling clamped tight around my chest.

When I hung up, I thought, *I should call the nurses' station. But how many transfers will I have to wait through before I can talk with the right person? I can't wait that long.* I prayed, *God, what's happening? Be with Don and help the doctors do the right things for him. God, help us all.*

I grabbed my coat and rushed off to the hospital. After a dash into town, I drove into the hospital parking lot. *Aren't there any spots left in this lot today?* When I finally parked the car, I rushed past people down the hospital's interminable halls to Don's room.

When I burst into his room that morning, my strong, vibrant, forty-year-old husband looked like an eighty-year-old man clinging to the edge of life. Don greeted me, but his words were garbled, and the right side of his face drooped severely. He looked confused and lethargic. The entire right side of his body lay on the bed as if it was dead; none of his muscles responded when he tried to move anything on that side.

I thought, *These are classic stroke symptoms!* I remembered what I had learned in my student nursing days and when I worked as a registered nurse before we had children.

Those first hours began to spin; cardiology and neurology specialists came in to examine Don, and nurses and technicians slipped in and out of his room. The doctors ordered more blood work, an electrocardiogram, a CT scan, and an angiogram to determine the condition of the blood vessels in Don's neck and head. When Don went off for his tests, he could not move himself, so four hospital staff slid him onto a gurney. I ached as I watched Don's helplessness.

I repeatedly thought how blessed we were that Don was at Mayo. Mayo Clinic is one of the world's most renowned medical centers. Experts cared for Don, using the best technology known at the time. Although I felt alarmed by Don's condition, I was confident in his care.

Only four days before, Don had returned from a trip to

Zaire in central Africa. Don loved his work as a psychologist. ı
also loved the freedom his own private counseling practice gave
him to make annual consulting trips to work with missionaries.
*I'm thankful he wasn't in a remote African hospital or all alone in a
Paris hotel room when this hit him,* I thought.

The doctors and nurses frequently asked Don, "What is
your name?"

He always responded, "Don Kvernen."

They asked, "Can you tell me where you are?"

That was a harder question, and Don's answers were
frequently confused. I sometimes heard frustration in his voice
when he could not answer the question. Other times my heart
sank as I heard him answer with confidence, oblivious of his
"mistakes."

Hospital staff checked Don's reflexes and other
neurological responses. When they pricked him with pins, he
responded only on his left side. An invisible line ran down his
midline, separating what he could feel or not feel.

During one exam, a neurologist asked Don to shut his eyes.
"Dr. Kvernen, I am going to move your right arm to different
places, and I want you to move your other arm to match that
same position." Each time the doctor gave instructions, Don
moved his usable arm but often put it in a different place. This
test showed Don had no *proprioception*, which meant he could
not sense the location of the parts of his body on the side affected
by his stroke.

When the staff asked him to move various parts of his
body, squeeze their fingers, or resist pressure pushed against

him, Don responded with his normal strength on his left but could not respond at all on his right.

Don looked like he was in a fog, and he slept a lot between his tests. When he woke, Don sometimes squeezed my hand and told me he loved me. At times I could grasp the spirit of what he said more than I was able to understand his garbled words. I wondered, *What will our future be?* Don was still alive, but grief and fear of the unknown overwhelmed me.

I debated, *Should I tell our boys right away? Should I bring them to the hospital? But if I go to pick them up from school, I'll have to leave Don for about an hour. What's best for the boys and for Don? Maybe I should wait and tell them about Don's stroke after some of the tests are completed.* I waited.

Even though no one could tell me yet the extent of what had happened to Don, I needed to tell his family what I knew. When Don left for his angiogram, I called his siblings. I asked his brother to break our bad news to his mom. Don's younger sister worked as a nurse a little over an hour from Rochester. When I called her, Lowie said, "I'll come right away!"

When Don went to the ER once in the past, my brother-in-law asked me, "Is someone there for you?" When this memory dawned on me, I called my dear friend Mary, and she came to join me until after Lowie arrived. Mary is a friend who could love and support me with her presence and a few words and not have to talk all the time. That is what I needed. I called other friends who each expressed their concern and promised to pray for us. Some came to visit.

That afternoon Don's neurologist called me into the

hallway, "We do not know if Dr. Kvernen will live. What are your wishes regarding life support?"

The doctor's blunt question hit me like a brick. I understood Don's condition was serious, but I could not even think what our choices were. Don and I had never seriously discussed those matters and had not yet written advance directives. I felt pressure to make decisions without anyone fully understanding the extent of Don's condition or what the future held. A weight of loss and uncertainty gripped my mind and body.

Between my tears, many thoughts raced through my head. *Oh dear, this is big. God, help Don! Help the boys and me! Am I going to be a widow? Will Jon and Josh grow up without their dad? What will Don be like if he survives this? Will Don recover to what he used to be? Will he ever work again?* The questions continued their barrage.

However, between the waves of grief, I also felt peace. Three years earlier when Don fractured his skull in a skiing accident, his ER doctor told us Don might die if the bleeding in his brain did not stop. Even though he lay there between life and death, we both experienced an amazing sense of calm. Since our relationship was strong, we did not suddenly have to make things right on his deathbed; Don knew his relationship with God was in order; and we both believed God was with us no matter what happened. Sitting with Don this time, I sensed the same paradox of turmoil and peace come over me.

Later, doctors assured us that Don's earlier skull fracture had no relationship to his stroke. Different factors caused the bleeding and it occurred in different areas of his brain.

My heart ached for our kids. Don had a close relationship

with our boys. They loved their dad. He always talked easily with them, demonstrated his interest in them, and expressed his love for them. In turn, they let him into their lives. I dreaded the pain they were about to experience.

Near the end of the school day, I called the high school and the elementary offices to explain our situation. I talked with Jon and told him, "Dad's still in the hospital, and something happened to his brain that has made him very sick. Auntie Lowie came down from the Cities, and she'll pick up you and Josh from school and bring you to the hospital. I'll tell you more when you get here."

I met Lowie and the boys after they came into the hospital. I still can picture our walk down that long hall, trying to prepare the kids to see their dad in his devastated condition.

Our family clung together around Don that sobering afternoon as each of us absorbed the weight of what had happened. I remember feelings of love, shock, and uncertainty. We hugged and quietly talked, ached, and at times silently sobbed. Don's room was in an older part of St. Marys Hospital; the dark curtains, the brick view, the cramped space, and the aging furnishings all added to the gloom that closed in on us. Brief moments of relief came when a few friends stopped by to hug us and tell us they loved us.

Late that afternoon, Jan Buckner, a physician friend of ours came to visit. While he was there, the staff neurologist called us out of the room to explain Don's test results. In helpless despair, I asked Jan, "Would you come with us to hear the news?"

My heart sank as I saw for certain the extent of Don's diagnosis of stroke. Don's angiogram showed that a huge area of his brain no longer received a supply of fresh blood and now just held dead tissue.

With their extensive medical experience, Dr. Buckner and Lowie understood Don's prognosis better than I did. In my shock, my knees felt as if they were about to buckle. Jan and Lowie held the boys and me up with their loving presence and tearful smiles. They did not need a lot of words to express their care.

I do not know how much Don understood when the neurologist explained Don's test results to him, but he appeared to at least comprehend the gravity of the situation. Lowie, Jon, Josh, and I gathered around Don's bed and held each other, and we quietly cried and processed our shock. Don slipped in and out of sleep. Between times, he tried to talk with us, but we had a difficult time understanding many of his words.

So far, shock and grief completely crowded out any thoughts of hope in my mind.

In the early evening, the hospital staff moved Don to the neuro ICU. Sadness crushed my chest as I saw him so sick and helpless, needing all those medical devices. Because the ICU staff limited the time we could visit, we went back and forth between Don and the friends and family who sat with us in the large family waiting room. Many people who loved Don were hurting. When his good friend Jarry left that evening, he walked slowly away from me down the hall and looked like he carried the world on his shoulders. We were nearing the end of a grueling day.

Thoughts continued to flood through my mind. *I love Don*

and I'm scared. If his condition deteriorates, I want to be with him. I don't want him to die alone! But should I stay with him tonight, or should I go home for our boys? I feel like I'm needed in both places. I'm about ready to collapse. If I become sick because I'm too exhausted, I won't be a help to anyone. I think I need to go home to sleep.

When I asked Don where he thought I should spend the night, he clearly told me to go home to sleep and care for our boys. The nursing staff assured us we could leave, and they would call if Don's condition worsened or he asked for us. So that first night, the boys, Lowie, and I reluctantly left Don in the care of the ICU staff. On one hand, I wanted to be with Don. But on the other hand, Don and the rest of us felt this was the right decision.

When I heard that more of our family planned to arrive in the middle of the night, I arranged for them to sleep at our neighbor's until morning. I fell into bed that night completely spent but woke up with a start in the middle of the night, my mind racing with all the possibilities ahead. I wondered, *Will Don ever lie here beside me again? What will his life be like for him?* I sobbed myself back to sleep.

Except for being a male, Don did not score at all on the list of risk factors for stroke.

- At age forty, he was relatively young.
- His blood pressure was normal.
- His cholesterol was normal.
- He had no family or personal history of heart disease, stroke, or *transient ischemic attacks* (TIAs or ministrokes).

- He had no medical conditions that might precipitate a stroke.
- He did not smoke, did not use alcohol or drugs.
- He was not overweight (at least not much).
- He was moderately active physically; he played racquetball two or three times a week and enjoyed other vigorous physical activities.

Don was diagnosed with a left *internal carotid dissection*; he had a tear with a clot in the internal branch of his left carotid artery at the top of his neck. This clot blocked the flow of oxygenated blood beyond that point to about half of the left side of his brain. Because each hemisphere of the brain controls the opposite side of the body, Don's right side was paralyzed.

Doctors can describe a stroke and its effects, but in about forty percent of stroke and TIA patients, a definite cause is not found.[1] So why did Don have his stroke?

One of Don's doctors later told him, "Perhaps during your flight home from Africa, you developed a clot in your leg. When you came home, the clot could have dislodged and passed on to your brain through a small opening in your heart called a *patent foramen ovale* (PFO) causing your stroke."

Another doctor refuted that. "A clot could not have caused the tear in your carotid artery. A tear must have occurred first, creating bleeding and a disturbance in the blood flow, which then caused the clot."

Still another doctor conjectured, "You may have had a small tear in your carotid artery, but the heparin you received

---

1 pfodoctor.org (accessed 2/20/11)

in the ER may have caused more extensive bleeding and damage."

Although there is no way to know the exact cause of his stroke, we know Don had a severe and disabling stroke some time during that night between March 18 and 19, 1991.

When our friends and family heard about Don's stroke, many sent cards and flowers. Flowers were not allowed in the ICU, so we took them home. Because of allergies, we put the bouquets in our garage on Don's new John Deere garden tractor and took a picture that he later enjoyed.

Both Don's and my family members came to visit us in the first days after Don's stroke. We needed them during those difficult days, and they needed to come. Later Don teased, "You came all that long distance to see me, but you wasted your trip; I don't even remember that you were here." I love Don's delightful ability to turn many situations into humor.

Laughter sometimes helped us endure our pain. Not only did our family help us bear the burden of our painful adjustments, they also shared humorous incidents with us.

One day as Don's two sisters, Bev and Lowie, and I returned to the ICU after lunch, someone in our packed elevator passed gas. Everyone stoically faced the front of the elevator without a change in their facial expressions. When we reached Don's floor, the doors opened and we stepped out. The moment the doors shut, we doubled over in hilarious laughter. This was the first time I experienced a sense of relief from that vice-like feeling in my chest that started the morning of Don's stroke.

Another day, Don's sisters went into the ICU to help Don

with his meal because he could not feed himself. While Lowie fed him small bites, Don repeatedly asked, "Give me some corn." But there was no corn. Because Don's speech was quite mixed up, they thought he was using the wrong noun for the vegetable, so Lowie gave him the peas again. This happened twice, and each time he ate what she gave him.

The next time Don asked for corn, Lowie said, "There isn't any corn on your plate."

He answered, "I can pretend." Don had lost a lot, but not his humor.

Lowie visited Don in the ICU one day and read some of his cards to him. Don said to her, "Put the cards in the right envelopes or they'll get mixed up." There were times his words and ideas were all confused, but other times like this he clearly expressed himself.

Two worlds pulled at the boys and me: Don's need for support to survive his stroke and our need to carry on with life. Our situation reminded me of when my father had his strokes. Although my sister and I dearly loved our dad, our mom felt we needed to continue our regular activities to help us cope with his impending death. One night I felt a strong desire to go to our civic orchestra practice, even though it was a particularly bad day. In that instance, playing my cello comforted me.

In addition to visiting their dad, our kids kept up with school, sports, and church activities, with dental and eye exams, a music contest, babysitting jobs, and outings with friends. While Don was still in the ICU, some dear friends took Jon with them on a college scouting trip. Routine helped carry the kids through the trauma in their lives.

After six days in the neuro ICU, Don moved to a private room on a general neurology floor. The staff told us Don needed to regain more strength before he could move on to the rehab unit. This news gave us our first ray of hope that Don might recover. Don's speech had not improved yet, and we had discovered that he could not read. However, he was becoming more alert and beginning to sleep less.

Don gradually started to come out of his fog. About ten days after his stroke, Don's cousin Dr. Gary Karlstad came to Rochester and stopped at the hospital to visit Don.

Don tells the story like this: "I thought, *Why is he standing here, when he lives way up in North Dakota? I couldn't figure it out. That is my first memory after my stroke.*"

I pieced together a story after a man Don knew from Rotary visited him one day. Their club had collected used medical equipment from the Rochester area to send to a hospital in Kenya. Don helped pack the shipping container right before he left for Zaire. During their conversation, Don's visitor must have mentioned that some hospital beds were still left at the warehouse where they packed the container.

The nurses told me that after his visitor left, Don talked with much distress about "the waterbeds." They could not understand what he was saying. When I came into his room that afternoon, Don tried to explain the waterbeds to me in a very agitated voice. The staff thought he might be having another stroke, so they sent him off for another brain scan. The scan did not show any new stroke activity. A few hours later, I finally figured out Don was talking about hospital beds from the shipment. This was an example of his *aphasia*; he said things differently than he thought them in his head.

Anomia was an aspect of Don's aphasia. This meant he could not name people and had great difficulty correctly naming things around him. He could not remember the names of any of our extended family members or friends except three couples who were significant in his life: Orien and Elaine Klath, Ronnie and Elenore Grinde, and Jarry and Linda Richardson.

Although Don knew Jon and Josh were our sons and could say both their names, he could not figure out which name to use for either of them. When he saw them, he said things that showed he knew exactly who each son was; he simply could not access their correct names in his brain.

Don could usually say my name but sometimes introduced *me* as his "husband." Several times when I came into his room, Don greeted me with, "Rosella stopped by to see me. Rosella. You know! r-o-s-e-l-l-a, r-o-s-e-l-l-a." I could hear his agitation grow when I did not understand him.

Almost every day, Don asked someone how soon he could move to the rehab unit. Near the end of his eleven days on the general neurology floor, therapists from the physical (PT), occupational (OT), and speech therapy departments came to his room, assessed him, and began their therapy plans. Don could not sit well in a wheelchair yet, so for his first sessions, they wheeled him on a gurney to the rehab department on the other side of the hospital.

What helped us cope and gave us hope:

- Friends and family assured us of their love and prayers.
- I went home for a good sleep at night while Don was in the hospital.
- Humor brought temporary release from our pain and stress.
- Our kids kept some normal routine in our lives.
- The hope of getting into rehab kept us going.

Chapter 2
Inpatient Rehab

Don moved to inpatient rehab seventeen days after his stroke. This change meant his doctors thought he was medically stable and had enough strength to profit from several hours of therapy each weekday. In his garbled words, Don told me, "Now that I'm here, I can start to get better." We talked of hope as he began this new stage of recovery.

The furnishings on the physical medicine and rehabilitation (PM&R) unit on 3-Mary Brigh of St. Marys Hospital were new and bright. As the April sun flooded through the large windows of his room, our spirits rose. I set out Don's plants, the cards, and artwork some children gave him. In his new double room, he had much more space and could visit with his roommate. A volunteer even came by with a cart of pictures and asked Don to choose what he wanted to look at on his wall.

On the weekend of his move, Don progressed to sitting in a wheelchair. From his first Monday in rehab, the hospital staff or I pushed him to his appointments in a wheelchair instead of on a gurney. I was a homemaker at the time, so I could go with Don to his therapy sessions. Each day Don was scheduled for two PT sessions, two of OT, one of speech, and one of recreational therapy (RT). Between therapy, doctors' visits, other miscellaneous appointments, meals, and his nursing cares, Don's scheduled activities filled most of his day. He had little time for visitors except in the late afternoon or evening.

The PM&R unit of the hospital treated patients with traumatic brain injury (TBI), spinal cord injury (SCI), stroke, and other neurological problems. Many patients there dealt with more than a quick health crisis and recovery; many patients and their families struggled to adjust to tragedies that permanently changed their lives. In rehab, the therapists tried to restore patients as much as possible to wholeness. Don talked with high hopes of making a full recovery.

Before their therapy sessions, twenty to thirty patients and family members crowded the rehab waiting room. Like Don, several patients waited with their paralyzed arms elevated by blue foam wedges on their wheelchair trays. The wedges were used to minimize the *edema* or swelling that tended to happen if a patient's hand hung down without movement. Some patients wore halos because of fractured necks. A few other patients lay waiting on gurneys.

Some patients were so sick or exhausted they could not talk. Others enjoyed chatting. Even at first when Don was quite sick, he talked with other patients, asking them about their families or talking about their progress. Although he mixed up his words, he made little encouraging comments.

Stroke patients struggle with heavy fatigue. Don strained in his rehab therapy and frequently hit the limit of his stamina, needing to stop and rest before he could continue. Between his scheduled appointments, Don sometimes asked to go back to his room and lie down, if only for a few minutes. However, his therapists told Don he needed to push himself to develop stamina.

At one of Don's family patient conferences, Dr. Lie and the other hospital staff members cried with us about a challenge we faced. We do not remember the issue, but Don and I have talked since then about how much their expression of concern meant to us. The rehab doctors, nurses, and therapists were not only competent and exceptional professionals in their fields of medicine, they were wonderful, kind people. They balanced compassion with teasing and motivation with comfort when they worked with Don.

Don made a significant choice as he settled into his rehabilitation. One day he said to me, "I didn't intentionally cause my stroke. It just happened, and I can't change that. I don't want to become bitter about it."

Don's choice of attitude was consistent with his personality. I was amazed he could make that decision so early in his illness. Don's resolution made a huge impact on his life and on our family. I watched his positive attitude help his disposition and draw people to him instead of drive them away. Don's model inspired the boys and me to choose the same approach. We all benefited from Don's wisdom.

Don and I agreed that we simply did not want to focus on bitterness and waste energy we could better apply to his recovery. We did not have to deny the pain; we just did not want to let our losses fester and control our lives.

Physical Therapy

When Don started physical therapy, he joined other patients who were also working to improve their mobility. Like Don, they had all acquired some sort of physical limitation that was usually more obvious than the cognitive problems many of them also faced.

The physical therapists (PTs) occasionally started their patients' therapy on their walk down the hall toward the gym. In the gym, some therapists took their patients to padded exercise tables at one end of the room. Others went to work on a set of parallel bars along the south wall of windows or on a short staircase that sat in the middle of the room. Before they could go home, patients had to be able to climb in and out of an old orange Mustang that sat nearby. Around the corner, patients practiced stepping up and down on a set of simulated curbs. Some patients worked on weight machines. The gym hummed with activity as therapists helped their patients use gym balls, colored Thera-Band strips, exercise equipment, and other assistive devices.

Staci, Don's physical therapist, specialized in treating stroke patients. This young woman's energy and smile showed she loved her work. I could see from the beginning that Don enjoyed his hour-long sessions with her each morning and afternoon. He responded with a smile of satisfaction each time she praised him for a bit of success. I was amazed, watching her motivate him with her expertise and her wonderful mixture of compassion and humor. She always had a positive attitude, and that matched well with Don.

When Don began physical therapy, he could not even roll

over in bed, much less sit up. He could not make his right side function at all. The muscles on his left side worked normally when he lay in bed. However, when Staci sat Don up, he grimaced with apprehension and his body tensed so much he could not even control his left side. He leaned way over to his left and backwards.

Staci explained to us that, like other stroke survivors, Don's perception of his center of gravity had become distorted. He could not judge the position of his body. He most likely felt like he was tipping over, falling off a ledge. She said it was natural for Don to fight for balance over his right side, the only part of himself he could feel.

As Staci tried to help him sit, Don burst out, "I'm going to fall!" or cried, "No! No! No!" When they stopped, Don told Staci in jumbled words, "I'm sorry! I know you want to help me, but this is scary! I want to work hard for you and get better. I'll try to do what you say." If Don could not express himself verbally, his tense body and his resistance clearly communicated his fear.

While the muscles on Don's right remained physically intact, his brain could no longer process the messages to make them work. Staci assisted Don to use the muscles that he could still control on the other side of his trunk. And as some of the muscles on his right side slowly recovered from paralysis, she helped him begin to use them. Staci worked hard to reteach Don the feeling of correct balance when sitting; Don worked hard, too.

Before he could walk, Don had to learn to stand. Staci buckled a wide gait belt around his waist to give her a sturdy grasp. With her support, he lurched to a stand, looking startled by his success. With his eyes full of terror, Don leaned with all his strength over his left side and clamped his left hand tight on Staci's arm. She had to shift Don, against strong resistance, to help him put weight on his paralyzed leg.

When Don stood, his five-foot-eleven, 180-pound frame dwarfed Staci who was not much over five feet tall. As she shifted his weight past his comfort zone, Don told her he was afraid he might fall and hurt himself or crush her.

"I haven't dropped anyone yet," she said smiling.

Don said he could not sense where his right leg was, or if it existed, unless he looked down to see it. He had to learn to trust Staci, as well as to trust his paralyzed leg.

Once Don could stand, he needed to learn to step on one leg at a time. Tom, one of the assistants in the PT gym, stood in front of Don to support him and reduce his fear while Staci knelt on the floor. Don's right ankle could not support him; whenever he exerted effort, muscle spasms turned the sole of his foot severely inward. Staci had to use both of her hands to stabilize Don's right foot when he shifted his weight onto it. When he stepped, she had to move his foot for him.

Tom walked alongside Don and kept saying, "Breathe, Don! Breathe!" Even from the sidelines, this was an intense experience to watch, and I held my breath along with Don.

When Don had "walked" about twenty-five feet, he hit his limit and had to sit down. But he grinned at me and said, "I'm beginning to walk! There's hope."

Staci ordered a custom-made *ankle-foot orthosis* (*AFO*) to stabilize Don's ankle. This plastic brace ran from just behind his toes to a flexible joint at his ankle and up the back of his calf to just under his knee. Two padded Velcro straps held Don's foot and lower leg in place. Staci removed the insole from his shoe so his foot and AFO could fit in his regular shoes. Initially Don did not want the AFO. "If I wear a brace, I feel like I'm admitting defeat."

Almost immediately after Don's AFO arrived, he realized how much it increased his mobility. Later, Staci ordered another AFO for him with a bump under the ball of his foot. Staci explained that since a little sensation had returned to Don's right foot by that stage of his recovery, when he stepped on the bump, it helped him sense where he placed his foot. When he started to use the new brace, Don said it helped.

When she began working with Don, Staci gave instructions using the words right and left, forward and backward, up and down. However, since Don could not understand or follow those instructions, she began to cue him. She demonstrated and physically helped Don shift his weight as she said, "Put your weight on this foot and move that one forward."

During some of those early days in PT, I slid a chair along a few feet behind Don for when he had to stop and rest. I was glad I could be there to see him make progress and to encourage him. Don told me he liked having me there, and the PTs never made me feel I was intruding. Although Don had suffered the stroke, I was hurting, too; I felt vulnerable. Their acceptance of me and of my presence helped me through that difficult time.

On one hand, Don's progress in PT was steady, but it seemed to come at a snail's pace. I vacillated between the hope we had and the discouragement I felt with his slow progress.

When I felt down, Don encouraged me; when he seemed down, I tried to encourage him. At times when we were both down, therapists or friends picked us up.

At first, Don held onto one of the parallel bars when he walked, but soon he graduated to a cane. Because vision was the primary sense Don trusted, he looked down whenever he stepped. However, Staci said, "We want you to develop good habits from the start, so look forward as you walk, not down. We'll hold onto you with the gait belt, but we don't want you to become *dependent* by hanging onto a person. You feel scared when you don't have anyone to hold on to; but we want you to use your cane in order to become *independent*."

Don held his cane in his left hand for two reasons. Obviously that was the only hand he could use. Secondly, his good leg could hold him, but he needed support when he stood on his paralyzed leg. Using the cane on the *opposite side* of his paralyzed leg helped him lurch less from side to side. Even then, Don walked with an uneven meter to his gait. He moved his good foot forward in perhaps one fourth of the time he took to move his paralyzed leg forward. That rhythm to his steps minimized the time he spent on the foot he could not feel.

After Don began to use the cane, he gradually passed several other significant milestones in his PT rehab. One month after his stroke, he lifted his right leg slightly up off his mattress for the first time. That improvement allowed Don to pull his leg forward, instead of only swing it forward from the hip. The following week, he walked 120 feet with help, learned how to shuffle sideways, and moved his right arm a tiny bit for the first time. These feats excited him. Progress came slowly, but Don continued to express hope for recovery. He said, "Maybe my body is waking up."

In order to become independent, Don had to learn to climb stairs. As he tackled this task, Don displayed his classic signs of fear. His body tensed; his paralyzed arm involuntarily contracted or curled up toward his face; his paralyzed leg contracted and became harder to control; he gripped whatever he was holding onto until his knuckles were white; and he held his breath when he made a particularly scary move.

Again he uttered, "No! No! No! No!" But Staci patiently helped him learn to climb the short staircase in the PT gym. We all cheered when he made it back down off the last step.

Don learned a jingle to help him remember how to approach steps. It said, "The good go up to heaven and the bad go down to hell." When Don climbed the stairs, he first stepped up with his good foot and then pulled himself up. When he went down, he swung his paralyzed foot over the edge of a step, then lowered himself until his foot landed on the lower step, and finally followed with his good foot.

Gradually Don increased his stamina and abilities. One day he said, "I can't believe I walked the entire hallway around the offices; I used to think walking across the room was impossible." I was glad I could be there to cheer him on in his accomplishments.

Although Don and his therapists worked hard in the PT gym, Staci, Heidi, Tom, and others said or did funny things that caused everyone to laugh. Sometimes Don instigated the laughter. One day early in rehab, Scott, a PT student, praised Don for something he had accomplished by saying,

"That's perfect!"

Don responded, "Or a reasonable facsimile thereof."

Many patients came to the PT gym with severe illness or injury that ravaged their bodies. I recognized the blank look of devastation and shock on the faces of their family and friends. After Don made steps toward recovery, I began to take more notice of the new people who shared our experience. Our short breaks in the gym gave us opportunities to chat. I was able to tell families, "That's how my husband was a few weeks ago. Things will improve for you, too."

Occupational Therapy

Kathy, Sue, and other occupational therapists (OTs) worked with Don on activities of daily living (ADLs). He had to learn to bathe and groom himself, to dress with just one hand, to toilet himself, and to make transfers between his bed and wheelchair.

The OTs tried many techniques to restore the function of Don's paralyzed arm. In one exercise, he strained to fold the fingers of his good hand between the fingers of his paralyzed hand, grasp some plastic cones, and move them from one side to the other in front of him. Because of the severity of his stroke, Don made almost no progress to recover the use of his right hand and arm.

Don's OTs also worked to improve his cognitive (thinking and reasoning) skills and redevelop his fine motor skills. One day I watched Don methodically sort a bowl full of nuts and bolts as his OT instructed. When he finished his task, the nuts and bolts appeared almost as mixed up in the two new bowls as in the original one. My heart sank.

On one of his school vacation days, Josh came with me to attend Don's therapy sessions. Don's OT asked him to put together a four-piece puzzle of a cow, but he could not. Josh was twelve years old and could easily have put that puzzle together even when he was two years old. I saw pain in Josh's eyes as he silently watched what his dad could no longer do.

Due to Don's difficulties with language and cognition, he at times looked frustrated, like he could not understand what his OTs wanted him to accomplish or why. Don said, "I know I've learned many things, but I have a hard time getting motivated in occupational therapy because I don't see as much progress as I see in PT."

Speech Therapy

Don almost completely lost his ability to read and write. Although he had earned a Ph.D., he could not recognize the letters of the alphabet. Don could recite the *abc*'s and his vision was good, but he shook his head in bewilderment when he looked at letters or words on a page. Dave, his speech therapist, worked with Don on speaking, reading, and on other cognitive exercises. Don struggled to find words. He regularly failed to retrieve the names for many everyday objects on the pictures Dave showed him or to identify words to match Dave's oral definitions.

Once in a while during therapy, Don recognized a word by sight, often the name of a food. But if a word did not come to him immediately, he had no way to sound it out or decipher it.

One day I asked Don, "What do you want to eat tomorrow? What should I mark on your menu?"

Don could see the menu in my hands as I sat next to him, and somehow he recognized the word spinach.

"I don't want that!" he said emphatically. He could not read the word aloud, but in this rare instance, he knew exactly what the word meant!

Don said he liked his speech therapist and his therapy sessions, but he made little progress over the time they met. As Don came to the end of his outpatient speech therapy, his therapist told him, "Don, you probably will never regain your ability to read." As we drove home that day, Don looked somber and said, "I have to learn to read before I can go back to work! I hope he's wrong." That was a sad afternoon for both of us. We both felt deflated.

Recreational Therapy

Don told people, "As a farm boy, I knew more about work than play. I was a poor football player in high school because I wished I could have gone out for a Coke with an opponent rather than tackle him. I never liked competition. I found more satisfaction when I helped and encouraged people. Before my stroke, I worked hard and enjoyed my job. I relaxed at home when I drove my tractor, built a deck or fort for the kids, or enjoyed other physical activities with our family. Recreational therapy did not excite me. I complained to Rosella about the games and crafts my recreational therapists (RTs) tried with me. Those activities were neither fun nor fulfilling for me."

Once in RT, Don made a clock by finishing some wood

and attaching a face and mechanism to it. Frustrated because he could not read time, he threw the clock away shortly after he brought it home.

Another time, Don made a wooden holder, cleverly designed so he could play cards with one hand. He did not like to play cards before his stroke, and afterwards he was unable to read or strategize. He did not keep that project either. I am sure Don's RTs gave him choices, but Don did not show much interest in his recreational therapy.

Don said he liked his recreational therapists, just not the activities. I must not have recognized the importance of RT either because I do not remember going with him to many of those therapy sessions. After he came home, Don struggled to find enjoyable recreation. Time dragged for him until he figured out that his favorite recreation was still visiting with people and encouraging them. He simply went back to what he did for fun before his stroke.

Dr. Lie, Don's wonderful physical medicine and rehab doctor, once commented, "A person's social support system is one of the better indicators of how well they can recover from a brain injury."

When Don talked his friend Bob Sinex into recording some of his stories for a future book, Bob summarized Don's words on this topic in the following way:

> My support system was amazing. Rosella and our
> two sons, our extended family, friends, our church
> family, and the amazing hospital staff all supported

me with their kindness and care. I could never have accomplished what I have without them.

Rosella was my rock. She loved me, encouraged me, and stuck by me. Rosella accompanied me during most of my therapy; we both drew strength from each other. She observed techniques that later helped when we worked on exercises at home. There were times she could figure out what I was struggling to say to my therapists.

After my stroke, our boys cared for me, instead of me for them. They supported me even though it must have been difficult. They were such good kids.

And then there was my friend Jarry Richardson. He was a busy psychiatrist; but during most of my days in the hospital, he carved out time before work to visit me and pray with me. Words can't express how much that meant to me.

Dignity seemed to vanish for Don during his rehabilitation. Many situations confused him. He told me how humbled and embarrassed he felt when he could no longer figure out simple tasks or care for his own personal needs. I ached when he told me these things and when I thought about how capable he used to be.

Before he reached the rehab unit, Don needed continuous urinary catheterization. The rehab staff had to determine if Don could sense when his bladder was full and if he could empty it completely when he urinated. They did not want his bladder to become over-distended and permanently damaged. During that time, the techs regularly catheterized Don. Although he did not like this, he tried to be good-natured, in contrast to his roommate who said horrible things to the techs.

Less than a week after he reached rehab, Don passed the bladder test and he progressed to a urinal. He said he felt embarrassed to have that on his bedside stand when friends came to visit. In the final stage of this process, a nurse or two, either men or women, hovered while he learned to use the toilet. He said they probably did not enjoy the experience any more than he did, but they treated him with respect and he tried to be pleasant with them. I can only imagine that learning to go to the bathroom at age forty was a humbling experience.

On the rehab unit, patients ate lunch and dinner in a common dining room. I saw Don's personality and his former profession come through as he interacted with the other patients. He comforted people, teased, or told patients he had seen them make progress that day. Don seemed to be energized by encouraging others.

While some patients were too sick to visit, others joked and laughed as they ate together. Some bantered, "You can't leave rehab until you can remove the plastic wrap from your bread with one hand." I watched them gain a sense of solidarity as they shared their difficulties and celebrated their accomplishments.

Our boys attended school during the day and came up to visit their dad in the rehab unit about every other night. The boys' teachers were supportive and flexible, knowing our circumstances. Some days our neighbors or the kids' school friends invited Jon and Josh over after school. I was glad Jon had his driver's license; he could now use Don's car.

Our kids' church activities provided a safe place where people loved them and knew what had happened in their lives. Our friend Mary once brought Josh and a few of his friends up to visit Don after their Wednesday night church activities. The kids may not have come by themselves, but coming as a group was easier and helped them understand Josh's family situation.

I had previously kept busy running our household and volunteering in several settings. After Don's stroke, many details of my life suddenly fell off my priority list, leaving Don and the boys as my main focus. I usually spent the school day with Don in the hospital but went home in the later afternoon to spend time with the kids and make supper for them. We went to visit Don many evenings, but as Don progressed, I sometimes stayed home after we ate to be with the boys or to take care of bills and other household tasks.

Since my childhood, playing piano and singing have expressed the depths of my sadness or joy. Some evenings I sat down at the piano and cried as I played. Words of songs, especially those we sang in church, comforted me—words that reminded me of God's love for me; that said God was never going to leave me; that told me because of God, I could face the future no matter what it brought. Those moments at the piano purged my pain and filled me with strength to go on.

Every morning after the kids left for school, I drove ten miles from the country to St. Marys Hospital in Rochester. My mind was so preoccupied that I soon learned to write my parking spot on the parking ticket and keep it in my purse, to avoid forgetting where my car was later in the day.

When I walked down the long halls to the elevators, my heart ached because of the changes in our lives. I ached for Don, for the boys, and for myself. But I also thought, *I wonder about the people I meet in these halls. I'm sure many of them have painful stories, too.*

Each day as I reached the third floor, a beautiful, profound painting welcomed me to the rehab unit. This work by Mangels depicted a young father in a wheelchair flanked by two young children. The joy in that painting always gave me hope.

What helped us cope and gave us hope:

- We anticipated improvement once Don was accepted into rehab therapy.
- Rehab professionals cared for us but also cared about us.
- Don chose not to waste energy on bitterness.
- It helped to joke with patients and staff.
- Therapists kindly pushed Don beyond his comfort zone to make progress.
- Don still retained his gift of relating with people.
- Loving family and friends surrounded Don and our family.
- Music expressed my pain and gave me comfort and strength.

Chapter 3

Going Home

At his first rehab patient care conference, the rehab staff decided Don could go home on an experimental day pass the following weekend. I am not sure if I was more excited or more scared by this news. Back in his room, Don and I talked about how he had not been home in over a month and about how excited he was at the prospect. It was going to be wonderful to be together as a family in our own home. I also looked forward to being alone with Don. I wanted to lie close to him when he took a nap on our bed.

However, I had seen how much care Don needed. *How are we going to transfer Don between the car and the wheelchair, get him into the house, use the bathroom…? Will our boys and I be able to care for all his needs?*

On our way home, Don asked me, "Have I ever been on this road before?"

We had driven that road hundreds of times, and yet he did not recognize it! *Oh my goodness, what a change from the last time we were together before his stroke!* When Don's cognitive deficits surfaced like this, they hit me harder than his physical limitations.

That afternoon, the boys and I pulled Don in his wheelchair backwards up the two steps from the garage into the house. He cried with happiness when we rolled him around for a quick tour. The trip tired both of us so much we took a nap shortly after we arrived home. To be close and together on our own turf lifted my heavy heart.

We had to maneuver his wheelchair through tight doorways and help Don transfer to our bed and to the toilet in a cramped bathroom; there were countless things to learn. As we ate our first meal together in a long time, we dared to hope our family could recover and move on from the painful changes of the last five-and-a-half weeks.

Although Don enjoyed his home visit, he looked exhausted by early evening when it was time to go back to the hospital. I was relieved I could take my new questions back to rehab the following week. We would have been overwhelmed to leave the hospital without further help.

The last weekend in April, Don came home on his first all-weekend pass. That Friday afternoon, our neighbor Russ helped me pull Don up from the garage into our entry.

Saturday morning I heard a noise in the garage. When I opened the back door, I found that Russ had built a wooden ramp for Don. I had not thought yet of how to solve that important issue! Since he had a relative who used a wheelchair, Russ knew what to do. He and others helped us in generous and creative ways, perhaps because of their own life experiences.

About thirty friends came to our house to celebrate Don's birthday on the Saturday afternoon of his first weekend pass at home. The kids played pool and Nintendo down in the family room while the adults laughed and talked upstairs. Don sat in his wheelchair as a focal point of the living room, his right arm elevated on a pillow. He grinned as he soaked in the fun and the many loving words of encouragement our friends gave him.

Don was forty-one years old but needed help with almost everything he did. Learning how to accomplish the simple functions of daily life at home became a major project for the whole family. I was proud of our boys. They generally flowed with the situation as if it was simply a normal part of life. Don often told people how much he appreciated the boys' and my help.

Back in the hospital, Don worked hard at his inpatient therapy each weekday. As we saw improvements, he talked about his hopes for a full recovery. At that time, Don believed whatever had not come back just had not "kicked in" yet, but I wondered. The hospital staff and our friends were always encouraging, and Don said he wanted to work as hard as he could.

The first Sunday in May, Don went back to church for the first time. His emotions ran high that morning and he cried a lot. When we talked about it later, Don said, "I cried when I saw the many people who had supported us; I cried when I realized how different my life was from the last time I had been in church; I cried at the words of songs; I even cried for no reason at all."

Uncontrollable crying, in either happy or sad situations, is common for brain injury survivors. When Don cried, people tended to dote over him. After he pulled himself together, he told people, "I feel embarrassed and frustrated when I cry like that. Don't worry, I don't feel as bad as I look." I heard that if someone changes the subject of conversation, it can help people like Don gain control in those emotional situations, but I felt unkind when I tried to do it.

Don had other uncontrollable reactions after his stroke. Every time he yawned, his paralyzed arm rose out in front of him almost as high as his shoulder. We were really excited until we saw it happen many times and finally believed what the medical staff told us; this was involuntary, uncontrollable movement which Don did not initiate. Although his muscles were all intact, he could not fire them at will, but sometimes they fired on their own.

On May 25, Don left rehab to go home permanently. He had been hospitalized more than nine weeks, seven of them in rehab. Since he was scheduled to begin outpatient therapy the following week, he still had a support system beneath him. Don had come a long way since his stroke, but he certainly had not made anything close to a complete recovery. Don's return home marked progress. But we had heard that whatever function did not come back early was less likely to return at all, so we wished he had recovered more.

Before Don moved home, Staci ordered one of the nicest wheelchairs available for him, since it looked like he might need one for a long time. Don thought someone had told him he would never walk again, but he was determined to prove that prediction wrong. He continued to use the wheelchair for long distances but less and less as time passed.

The Tuesday after Memorial Day that year, Don started weekday outpatient rehabilitation therapy. His daily sessions of PT, OT, and speech therapy continued until late June. Gradually his rehab dwindled until the first week of December when he had his last day of therapy at the Saint Marys Hospital Physical Medicine and Rehab Unit.

Don and his therapists had all worked hard. He had come far, but there is a limit to what insurance will pay, and he had hit a plateau. Don was on his own to practice what he had learned and adjust or compensate for his remaining losses. Not accepting that his losses might be permanent, he still talked with high hopes of proving people wrong and making a full comeback. The therapy staff encouraged him to keep working.

When Don came home from the hospital, he took Coumadin as an *anticoagulant*, a medication with blood thinning properties given to prevent the formation of blood clots and further strokes. In those first weeks, Don frequently returned to Mayo Clinic to check his *prothrombin times*, a test of the blood's ability to clot. Those blood levels proved tricky to balance. While he was on Coumadin, Don had to be careful not to cut or bruise himself because he might bleed uncontrollably. Within weeks, Dr. Rohren, Don's primary care physician, discontinued the Coumadin and prescribed one aspirin a day. He told Don that he needed to take aspirin indefinitely for its blood-thinning properties.

After Don came off the Coumadin, he could resume shaving with a razor blade. He said he was anxious for a close shave after using the electric razor for many weeks. The day before we went to our July 4 family camp, Don shaved for the first time with a blade. When I asked him if he needed help, he told me he was sure he could shave himself.

Well, Don had lost some coordination with his stroke.

When I came back into the bathroom, he sported about a dozen little horizontal bleeding slices all over his face. I saw that he held the handle down, but then he pulled his razor sideways instead of down! On top of the stress of figuring out how to travel with a bath bench, a wheelchair, and other supplies, Don was quite a sight. He had long dark scabs on his face our entire time at camp.

Don's therapists had drilled into him, "Don, you're the only one who can be responsible to protect your paralyzed arm. If you lie on your arm or if it gets caught in something, you could develop serious troubles. You need to always know where your arm is and keep it safe."

One night not long after he came home from the hospital, Don suddenly woke me from a deep sleep, uttering, "Where's my arm?!" At the same moment, I felt his left hand reach over to me, grab my left arm, and plop it on his chest. He found an arm; it just was not his.

Before Don's stroke, he regularly played racquetball with his friend Kel. After the stroke, Kel offered to take Don out for lunch every Friday. Don's face lit up each week as he anticipated this bit of independence and a fun time with a good friend. When Don came home, he usually told me that he and Kel went to the same Chinese restaurant, sat at the same table, and ordered the same thing, frequently from the same waitress.

Twenty years later, Don says, "I'd love to play racquetball again with Kel, but so far we just eat instead." They eventually diversified both their destination and menu.

Many of our friends told us how they were profoundly shocked by what happened to Don at such a young age. Some said, "After we saw what happened to you, we've had to reassess our priorities, our finances, our faith, and especially our marriage."

Before his stroke, Don treated the clients in his psychology practice with absolute confidentiality. When we met them socially, he did not identify them as clients. However, if I sensed someone perhaps knew Don, I quietly slipped away to give them the opportunity for a brief chat. After his stroke, a number of Don's former clients came up to us in public and told him, right in my presence, how much he had helped them. Encouragement like that was the best medicine he could get.

As Don ventured out more in public, friends and even strangers offered to help him. They hurried to open a door for him or carried his food to a table. Almost everywhere he went, he ran into considerate people. Since Don's cane and his labored walk alerted people to his disabilities, they readily helped him and were not surprised when they observed his cognitive problems.

We met other people with traumatic brain injuries who had significant cognitive deficits but no outward physical signs. They told us how people expected them to function normally and were judgmental and demanding of them. Because Don's disability was obvious, people were usually quite understanding toward him.

Don held his cane in his left hand, so when people offered to help him out of a car or up from a chair, they naturally reached for his right arm. Don's therapists taught him he needed to protect his shoulder. Because his muscles no longer held his right shoulder joint firmly in place, people might unwittingly pull his shoulder out of joint and cause long-term or even incapacitating pain for him.

Although Don appreciated help when he needed it, when people reached out to help him, he often blurted out, "Don't touch it!" He quickly apologized and later told me how embarrassed he felt by his intense reaction. Don concluded that the best way for people to help him was to first ask if he needed the help and, if he agreed, to offer him their right arm so he could hold onto them with his left arm.

That summer of 1991, we continued to figure out how to do many things for the first time. We tried to move toward the life we had before Don's stroke and figure out our "new normal." In mid-August, we made our first big trip to see family in North Dakota. By the time we started our drive, I was already tired from packing all our stuff. Our doctor said that in order to avoid developing a clot from inactivity, Don should exercise his legs at least every two hours. With those extra breaks, we stretched our former six-hour drive into eight hours.

We had not anticipated the difficulty of finding a restroom for Don. Both for Don's and for the boys' dignity, I did not want to make the boys help Don go the bathroom. However, fast food restaurants and large gas stations had multiple stalls in their restrooms; I could not go in to help him. We had the same problem at rest areas. Finally, we found small gas stations where I could go into a restroom with Don to help him.

Our boys grew up suddenly when Don had his stroke. Almost overnight they stopped fighting. On their own, they realized that how they looked at each other over breakfast was not cause enough for a disagreement. I was thankful I no longer needed to deal with that old bickering that is common to young siblings. Though our kids experienced many losses, they rarely complained or expressed resentment for our situation.

Our son Jon took advantage of an opportunity and learned to pop wheelies with Don's wheelchair. As I watched Jon, I sometimes wondered, *Oh dear, are we going to have two family members with brain injuries?* But he never fell.

As we settled back into life, Don and I wanted to support our boys in their activities, to attend their concerts and sporting events at school. However, we quickly realized we could not handle more than home games. When we went to those games, I had to push Don in his wheelchair over bumpy grass to reach the baseball field. Several times, he almost catapulted out of his chair when his front wheel ran into a hole. In those years, there was no handicapped access to the fields. I struggled because keeping up with our kids was such a priority for us.

Some homeowners who lived near the playing fields for our boys' high school put up No Parking signs and signs that told spectators not to walk through the area to the fields. I understood their desire for privacy, and yet I felt hurt by the message of those signs because I had to work so hard to take Don to the games. However, we were grateful for Don's handicapped parking sticker and for the accommodations that were made for people with disabilities in many other settings.

People expressed their love and concern for us while Don was in the hospital, as well as after he came home and we settled into our new life. They cared for us through their visits, cards, gifts, kind deeds, and prayers for us. Many of the people who helped us were our friends, but some were even strangers. Don could not say most of his friends' names at that time, and he still cannot, but neither Don nor I will ever forget how much their support and kindness meant to us.

What helped us cope and gave us hope:

- Mayo offered Don practice home visits from rehab.
- Friends and neighbors helped us with practical needs.
- After Don moved home, further outpatient rehab eased our transition.
- Rehab therapists encouraged Don to keep on working after his therapy ended.
- When we traveled, we found small businesses with individual restrooms where I could help Don.
- Our sons quit their sibling squabbles, and we all pitched in to help each other.
- We were able to ease back into watching our kids' activities.
- Friends continued social contact with us and expressed their love.

Chapter 4
Feeling Letters and Numbers

Don's stroke left him functionally illiterate. He said, "I can see words clearly, but they make no sense to me. I'm frustrated and humiliated that I can't read."

Kay Hawley, a woman from our church, heard that Don had lost his ability to read. Not long after Don started his rehab, she invited me out for lunch. We chatted with Don a few minutes before she and I walked to a restaurant near the hospital. While we ate, she told me some things her family had done to help her father recover after surgery for a brain tumor.

She explained, "I work with the Dyslexia Institute in Rochester and use the Orton-Gillingham teaching method. In addition to the usual visual and auditory fundamentals, this approach emphasizes *phonetics* (the study of speech sounds) and *kinesthetic learning* (learning or developing pathways in the brain by physical action and doing or feeling). I have no medical background, but Dr. Samuel Orton based his work on similarities he recognized in his dyslexic patients and his stroke patients. When Don finishes his therapy, I am willing to try to help him relearn reading and writing skills, if you'd like. I can't guarantee results, but I know the method couldn't harm him."

When I told Don about my conversation with Kay, he said he wanted to try her method after his therapy ended. Kay's offer represented a window of possibility.

Don was so busy with rehab that I let the idea slip to the back of my mind. As the months passed, his progress in speech therapy was slow, and we felt discouraged. After he moved home, Don said he longed for the mental stimulation he used to receive when he read books about his interests. He could not read for information or entertainment. He could not even read his Bible.

Almost seven months after Don's stroke, in October 1991, I called Kay. "May Don and I talk with you again about tutoring him? After next week, his speech therapy will be cut back to only once a week. They do not see much hope for Don to read again. In effect, he has to go home and adjust, but we hope he can somehow still improve his reading ability."

Kay invited us to her home. After lunch, she explained her method to Don and answered our questions. When she finished, Don and I read the look in each other's eyes and nodded. I said to Kay, "We want you to tutor Don. We want you to try to help him relearn the reading and writing skills he has lost."

Kay later told us she spoke that evening with her daughters, who were physical therapists, and both had said, "If you start, Mom, don't give up for at least five years." They had seen what stroke patients could achieve *if* they faithfully continued their exercise after their formal therapy ended when their insurance companies quit paying for it.

Don and Kay began their grueling tutoring sessions. They worked for an hour three times a week at Kay's kitchen table. Once Kay began to teach Don with the Orton-Gillingham method, he began to make his first recognizable progress toward reading.

I drove Don to his tutoring sessions, and by periodically sitting in on his early lessons, I learned how to help him practice at home. Other times, I waited for Don in Kay's living room as I fought exhaustion. She offered me a pillow and afghan and encouraged me to take a nap on her couch.

Although Don could race through reciting the alphabet, he could visually recognize and verbally pronounce the sounds of only four vowels and six consonants when Kay made her first assessment. He could not even do that consistently. As Kay taught, she *always* stimulated the kinesthetic pathways in Don's brain; she encouraged him to trace letters in a pan of uncooked rice with his left index finger, or "feeling finger." She also asked him to feel his mouth, tongue, and lip position when he produced sounds.

In her *visual drills*, Kay showed Don flashcards with letters. After he told her the name of the letter he saw and its sound, he traced the letter in rice. In *auditory drills*, Kay said the name of a letter and its sound, and before seeing the card, Don wrote the letter in rice. As he wrote the letters, he could both see and feel them in the rice. She gradually added more letters to these drills.

At Kay's house, Don traced his letters in a beautiful wooden tray his friend Dick made for him. At home we put the rice in a jellyroll pan. After Don wrote a letter, he shook the pan to erase it. Don had to learn to trace letters with his left hand because his previously dominant right side was paralyzed. Don initially practiced pencil grasp and letter formation of manuscript letters, both upper and lower case.

Kay's lessons always followed a sequential and repetitive format: a review of previously introduced material, a visual drill, an auditory drill, and later blending sounds, spelling, and reading.

Kay pronounced sounds and words very precisely when she worked with Don. When she said letter names, she did not pronounce a *schwa* sound after the consonants. When she said the sound for the letter *f,* she said the unvoiced consonant sound, not "fa" as in the first syllable of "fa-miliar." She said the nasal sound of *m* with lips together, not "ma" like the first syllable of "ma-jestic."

After many months, Don relearned the entire alphabet. Although he eventually learned all the letters, *b, d,* and *p* challenged him. Kay suggested that since the letter *b* was drawn with a downward stroke and a circle at the bottom, Don's clue could be "bat and ball." When he had difficulty naming the letter *b* on a flashcard, we said the sound (not the name) for *b* and/or "bat and ball." Similarly, the cues for the letter *d* became the sound for *d* and "drum stick." Kay taught Don to draw a drum and on the right side an upright stick.

When Kay started cueing Don for the letter *p* by saying "*p* in the pool," you can guess what came to his mind. The aids for those tricky letters helped Don, even though he never got past his first impression of that particular little hint for the letter *p.*

As Don learned the letters, Kay began to help him blend them together, for example, *fl, dr, st...* He had to learn digraphs (*sh, ch, ck...*) and trigraphs (*tch, dge...*). I relearned, along with Don, that there are seven ways to spell the long sound of *a,* eight ways for long *e,* six ways for long *i,* six ways for long *o,* and five ways for long *u*. Don also learned the multiple ways each vowel and some consonants can be pronounced. As Don progressed, Kay eventually added prefixes, suffixes, and root words to his lessons.

Later Kay taught Don cursive letters, but manuscript letters worked the best. Kay teased, "Don, your handwriting is probably more legible now than before your stroke." She was right. As he progressed, Don moved on from the pan of rice to trace on the table with his finger if he faltered, or later on his leg or in the air.

Don had to go way back to study early elementary reading skills, learning phonics all over again. However, when he was a child, he learned in a fraction of the time he needed to relearn skills after his stroke. As a child, Don learned to read with the Scott Foresman (Dick and Jane) primers. When his sister Bev loaned him some copies, Don and Kay read through them. He said it was fun to see those old books again.

Don struggled to learn to read again. He and Kay worked steadily through their entire hour together; he usually looked tired by the time he left her house. However, many times he said something like, "That was a good workout. I'm making progress." Or he grinned at me in the car and said, "I did the best I've ever done today."

I did not have to ask Don to practice at home; he initiated those sessions. I could tell that learning to read was one of his highest priorities along with learning to walk. Even though Don's progress was slow, it was steady over time. He still talked with hope about going back to work after he learned to read.

During his daily practice at home, Don strained for answers and needed prompts. The look on his face of intense focus revealed his frustration. He sometimes responded to my cues with comments like, "I'm trying!" At such times, I felt he was directing that frustration toward me. I filled the roles of wife, mom, nurse, financial director, taxi driver, cook, and teacher. Teaching was the most unnatural and stressful of my tasks.

When some friends offered their help, Kay agreed to teach them how to work with Don on the practice he needed to make progress. His friends not only helped Don; they also gave me treasured time alone to do whatever I wanted for an hour. Don seemed to respond to their direction with less agitation than he did to mine. I felt relief from no longer being his sole practice teacher.

When Don talked about how his friends had helped relieve stress on our relationship, he quoted a college professor who said, "When you have sugar for breakfast, and sugar for lunch, and sugar for afternoon tea, you know you're bound to puke sometime." That sounds a bit crude, but we both needed a break from each other.

A friend Randy Harmison helped Don for a while but later moved away. Art Maley, another retired friend, worked with Don and meticulously followed Kay's instructions. When Art returned to work, Don worked with Marv Rylander and Bob Sinex. These retired IBMers spent countless hours helping Don improve his reading skills. When the men left, Don always thanked them for their kindness and for making time to help him.

There were times when Don grasped the meaning of a word by merely seeing it, but instead of saying it, he said a synonym or maybe its antonym. Don once read a word as "sister," followed by "brother." When encouraged to sound it out, he finally correctly read it as "daughter." Don sometimes read "summer" as "winter," "Wednesday" as "Friday," or "Germany" as "France." He knew in his mind what the word was about, such as a season, day of the week, or a country; he even knew where a country was located on a map. However, he named a word that was not at all phonetically related. Don was oblivious of his error. With his aphasia, he could not spit out what he wanted.

Don studied for a few years before he could read complete sentences without stumbling. After he read eight or ten words at a slow, steady speed, he faltered as though he ran out of gas. A similar thing happened when he read for forty-five minutes or an hour; suddenly he tired, stumbled more, and had to quit.

Marv came every Thursday for many years to help Don with reading. They joked and chatted over something to eat and drink; then Don read to him from a magazine or book that interested him. When Don stumbled on words, Marv patiently helped him sound them out.

In early 1996, four years into their working together, Kay tried an experiment with Don's paralyzed right hand. She said, "Don, I am going to support your lower arm, and after I guide your finger to write something, I want you to tell me what we wrote. Close your eyes so you won't have any visual clues, only kinesthetic ones." Don was able to give the correct verbal response as they traced individual letters and spelled one-syllable words.

Kay added another component to this exercise. When they traced with his right index finger, she asked Don to reproduce letters with pen on paper, using his left hand. I was surprised to see how his proprioception had improved. However, Don never regained movement with his right hand.

Kay has said, "My work with Don brought me joy, frustration, blessings, fatigue, concern, reliance upon ideas that were a gift from above, and the pleasure of experiencing success with a dedicated student who truly understands that learning is a lifetime joy."

Don continued his tutoring with Kay for over ten years, meeting with her less frequently near the end. He eventually learned to write complete sentences, although he continued to make many spelling errors. Some of his writing examples are included at the end of this chapter. About eighteen years after his stroke, Don quit his practice sessions with friends. He has since lost some of his confidence, and he no longer likes to read aloud.

There have been times when Don has jumped to the wrong conclusion about what he read. A few years ago as Don was reading the newspaper, he saw a picture of someone he recognized and said, "Oh dear, did you see that he died?" When I looked at the paper, I had to tell him, "No, John didn't die; he earned a promotion at his job."

Don made phenomenal progress to reach the point where he could read silently for enjoyment. He now understands a significant portion of what he reads to himself, is able to use a pocket calendar, can understand most short notes I leave for him, and writes notes and letters. We are thrilled by the progress Don has made, especially when we think that at first he could not read anything. He once said, "When I couldn't read, I felt shut out from much of the world I enjoyed before my stroke. I felt frustrated and stupid when I couldn't read. Now I can read, at least to some extent. Reading helps me pass the time and gives me ideas to think about."

Math

As a result of Don's stroke, he became completely unable to tell time, understand numbers he heard, say numbers correctly, or frankly do anything with numbers. A classic example of Don's confusion with numbers happened when he was still in the hospital. Since our son Jon did not have a job at the time, I said to Don, "Jon wants to go to his prom. How much money do you think we should give him?"

Don said, "We should give him a thousand dollars."

I jumped in, "I think Jon will like that idea a lot, but I bet you mean a hundred dollars."

Don worked with numbers in rehab, and I worked with him hundreds of times on just the numerals 1, 2, and 3, but he made no progress. He still could not make sense of them.

TouchMath

When we talked with Kay about Don's difficulty with numbers, she suggested, "I think we should try TouchMath to help you learn your numbers and basic arithmetic skills. With this multisensory program, dots or TouchPoints are placed strategically on each numeral and counted aloud as they are physically touched or tapped with a pencil or finger. Some TouchPoints on the numerals 6 through 9 have a dot with a circle around them. These are double TouchPoints and they are touched and counted twice." (See Glossary and Figure 1.)

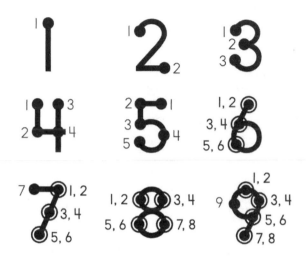

Figure 1. TouchMath Diagram[1]

Once a kinesthetic element was introduced into the process, Don began to read numbers within a few weeks. He practiced seeing, reading, hearing, and feeling the number of dots and soon had a way he could figure out what to call the numbers he saw on a page. He needed that method to open up his thought processes because depending only on his sense of vision was not enough.

I thought, *This is incredible!* I had watched how the kinesthetic input gradually helped Don learn to read, but this happened in no time at all, right in front of my eyes.

Don said, "We have to tell other people about this. I'm sure there are other people out there who have lost hope like I did, who could also be helped by this method."

Dick Tenley, another retired IBM friend, offered to help Don with math. Kay taught Dick the basics of TouchMath. After Dick taught Don to read and write the numbers and understand what they represented, he taught Don simple addition and subtraction and eventually progressed to simple multiplication and division. Dick played number games with Don; helped him work with money; worked on time, dates, Don's phone number, and address; taught him to use a calculator; and basically did anything simple he could think of with numbers. Each week Dick left homework for Don to finish before the next Thursday.

After more than seventeen years of Dick's weekly visits, Don decided he had hit a plateau, so he offered Dick retirement. Don used to tease Dick, "You come just because I laugh at your jokes and Rosella makes you a cup of coffee." But I am sure Dick came because he knew how much his help meant to Don.

Twenty years after his stroke, it is still hard for Don to understand how he can confuse his numbers when he thinks he has them right in his mind. However, once in a while he is right and I am wrong. Since I do not remember numbers well and Don cannot say them accurately, we often run into problems.

Punctuality ranks very high on the list of qualities Don values. He likes to arrive at an event twenty minutes early. If we talk about what time we need to go somewhere, he may nod, but later I realize he has not processed the information. Don sometimes thinks he understands and yet rushes to get ready an hour early. He frequently says, "I'll leave in an hour," when he means half an hour. If I cannot write a time down for him, I simulate the hand of a clock with my finger, but it works best if I write a time on paper for Don to see. He manages his time well if he can read it in his pocket calendar.

When Don hears a number, he usually begins to count, one finger at a time on his left hand. However, that technique generally leaves him confused. Even though it seems only slightly different, if I hold up the correct number of my fingers all at once, he seems to understand better. When I do not have paper and pen handy, it seems to help Don if I write a number in the air. Don's visual processing is much better than his auditory processing and his speech; he understands numbers best when he can see them.

Don loves to tell people about one of his college friends who farms thousands of acres in North Dakota. Even though I do not remember the exact number of acres, I know he is frequently off, not only on the numeral, but by a decimal or two in either direction. At those times I say, "I think you are a little high (or low)."

If I question the accuracy of a number Don quotes, he sometimes frowns at me and argues, "No, I know I'm right." I feel rotten if he says that when we are with people. I try not to always correct him, but I have a hard time knowing when I should step in or when I should just let an error go.

Later when we are alone and talk about such an encounter,

Don says, "I'm sorry I was harsh. I want to be accurate. You need to correct me." Don's aphasia frequently puts stress like this on our marriage. Again and again we have to forgive each other and go on—until the next time. These struggles will always be a part of our lives.

One of Don's friends with a brain injury tends to preface what he says by the fact that he gets things mixed up. I wish Don did that more. It boggles my mind to realize that after all these years, Don still does not grasp the depth of his aphasia, that what he says can be such an entirely different choice of words from what he means to say.

When Don's aphasia causes him to say something quite incorrectly, I feel bad for him. If he knew what he actually said, he might be embarrassed. I honestly think I feel more conscious of how those moments reflect on Don than for how they reflect on me. I do not care how I look, but Don is dear, and I want him to feel dignity. However, I suppose the matter of whose embarrassment I feel could be up for debate because Don is unaware of his language mistakes.

Even though I have described many of Don's struggles that persist, he has made enormous progress—from being completely unable to read or do math at first to functioning as well as he does twenty years later. I hate to think where Don would be without the Orton-Gillingham teaching method, TouchMath, and the many people who have helped him.

What helped us cope and gave us hope:

- A tutor for dyslexic students taught Don to read,

using the Orton-Gillingham method. Its multisensory approach gave Don his first significant progress in reading.

- The TouchMath method of learning unlocked numbers for Don.

- Friends helped Don with his reading and math practice, giving him a fun social connection and me a break from my many responsibilities.

- Because Don processes numbers he sees more accurately than what he hears, he copes by using a pocket calendar.

Wednesday, February 16, 1994

Dear Marv

Marv, this is the first day
I have remembered marved
Mamed, forved it is really somthing
Thang you fourve patient.

Spelling will also improve.
It is when when we consitler whear
camed from. Thanct four hanhanging
hanging in thair,

skincerly,

Don

Wednesday, February 16, 1994

Dear Marv,
Marv, this is the first day
I have remembered Marv's
name. For it is really something.
Thank you for being patient.
Spelling will also improve.
It is when we consider where (I)
came from. Thank (you) for hanging in there.
Sincerely,
                Don

Here is another example of a letter Don wrote by hand, accompanied by my translation. He sometimes leaves spaces for names he wants me to fill in for him. The love, gratitude, and details in the letter are quite typical of Don's letters.

, 06

Dear   ,

May you have a very have Berthday. We are fine. Josh and Beth are gething. Ready to start school this fall. Josh will find a jove and start school lather,

Svea will marry next month. We aree vory have for her. It is so sal that Jon died yet we are so have for his new wife, Svea hustund men is so have and it is foon to see him excited.
I said a wants to ceape us as mouch in volved. That is so neat.

There are soo many that that I apreciate in you. You never lied. You were alwiss anoist. That is a temands gift. The power fole influence that has had on me is harde to pouch in words

Some time I wish you were closser so we could sit down and talk. I have nothing brofound to say I simpaly would love to sit and talk.

Now is   doing? I fell so pad to wach him trying to get the medison set just right.

Hi to   .

May you get some raine to.

Again have Berthday.

Love,

Don

My translation of Don's preceding letter:

Aug.'06

Dear Orien,

May you have a very happy birthday. We are fine. Josh...
Beth is getting ready to start school this fall. Josh will find a job
and start school later.

Svea will marry next month. We are very happy for her.
It is sad that Jon died yet we are so happy for Svea to have a
new husband. Svea's fiancé is so happy and it is fun to see him
excited. She said she wants to keep us as much involved in their
lives as we have been. That is so neat.

There are so many qualities that I appreciate in you. You
never lied. You were always honest. That is a tremendous gift.
The powerful influence that has had on me is hard to put in
words. Sometimes I wish you were closer so we could sit down
and talk. I have nothing profound to say. I simply would love
to sit and talk.

How is Mary [Orien's daughter] doing? I feel so bad to
watch her trying to get the medicine set just right.

Hi to Elaine [Orien's wife].

May you get some rain too. [These friends are farmers
and it had been dry for the crops.]

Again, Happy Birthday!

> Love,
>
> Don

Don wrote this note to me October 10, 2006, after we had a
"discussion." It shows his sensitive spirit.

Rosella,
I am sorry I am not always so nice.
I am responsible to be nice. Forgive me.
Thank you for being you. You have to put up with a lot and
I fail to be nice. I want to improve in this area yet I will fail,
I am sure. I will still try to do better.
Love,
Don

Chapter 5

Communication

Words and ideas were the tools of Don's profession. When he spoke, he communicated thoughtfully and clearly. But for almost two decades, Don has struggled with aphasia—his difficulty with language. Although he has improved considerably, he still mixes up words.

Don's *expressive aphasia* impedes his ability to make his words and ideas understandable to others. It shows up if he says, "I'll come at two o'clock," but he is pointing to four o'clock on his calendar. He may say, "No," when he means, "Yes." It is hard for both of us to know if what he says is really what he means.

Don's *receptive aphasia* hinders his ability to understand words he hears or reads. An example of this might be if someone tells him, "Mike and Sue are expecting their first grandchild." Don may nod and say, "Good for them." But later he tells me, "Isn't it good that the ones who moved to a new house are going to have a grandchild?"

I have to explain, "It isn't the couple who moved; it's the couple we went to the concert with a couple weeks ago." I ask Don to say something else that describes them to be sure we are talking about the same people.

Even if Don understands what people say, he cannot

summarize a conversation or retell a joke. I have learned there is no point in asking Don to repeat a sequence of details. He says, "It's too hard for me to tell it to you."

Don does not always understand what we say, but at times he does not actually hear because of some hearing loss he acquired years ago. In addition, he frequently expresses his thoughts differently than he intends, or he believes he said something but did not say it aloud. I do not always express myself clearly, and now and then I cannot remember what was said, or he may not remember. As Don says, "We're a wreck!"

Unless you have lived with brain injury, you cannot imagine how many times we miscommunicate each day. To give an example, here is a real conversation Don and I had one night:

I came into the house and Don said, "You need to call the one in the second house."

Since I usually check things out to confirm details, I said, "Did Kim call?" I thought to myself, *Although Don has a hard time with names, Kim lives in the second house, and he sometimes recognizes her name.*

Don said, "No."

I asked, "Was the person who called from the house right next to ours?" I usually do not use names, but instead say something to describe the people.

"No."

I pointed back in the direction of the second house again and tried coming from a different angle. "Did Molly's mom call?" Don can occasionally come up with Molly's name.

"No, not her."

"Was it the people who added a room on the back of their house last summer?" I was at the third house around the cul-de-sac.

"No."

We stood in the kitchen, and I had been pointing out our window at the houses. At this point, Don pointed to the fourth house.

I asked, "Did someone call from the house where the front light is on?"

"Yes, that's the one," Don said.

As I dialed, I debated in my mind what I should say. How vague or exact should I be? I debated if I should say, "Don said someone in the neighborhood called for me. Did you call?" But Don was standing right there, listening to what I said, and he had confidently and visually, not just verbally, confirmed what he said. So I tried to uphold his dignity and went with the exact rather than the vague.

When our neighbor answered the phone, I said, "Hi, this is Rosella Kvernen. Don said you called."

The neighbor replied, "No. I didn't call; and my wife's been gone all evening, so I don't think she called either."

I went back to the third house and called them. This time I took the vague approach like I should have before. "Did you call earlier?" I asked.

"Yes, I called," Julie said. "I'm wondering if you can give me some dates you're available for the neighborhood Christmas party."

Bingo!

Don remembered that a neighbor called, but then our communication broke down. We usually continue until we discover the details Don wants to tell me, although the process can exhaust both of us. As in this case, we can go confidently down a wrong path and have to retrace our steps before our facts are straight. Sometimes we hit the target quickly, and other times we need many spirals of conversation. Every day we play our guessing games.

One of the most common vocabulary errors Don continues to make, whether he is reading or speaking, is to mix up pronouns. He has no idea when he confuses "he" for "she," "him" for "her," or "you" for "me." Even when he stops to think, he cannot figure out which pronoun to use. Our family and friends have grown used to this; we often continue a conversation as if nothing is wrong and try to figure out from the context what Don means.

Don may say to me, "She can't meet you for dinner tonight." After some questioning, I discover he really means his friend cannot meet Don for lunch the following day.

When I am uncertain about whom Don is talking, I usually ask if the person is a man like him, pointing to Don, or a woman like me, pointing to me. After we figure out the gender, I move on to describe individuals I might suspect. I may pass over people and have to come back to them because Don votes them down the first round. When we finally figure out the person Don is talking about, we find that other parts of the conversation are mixed up as well. With such vast potential for confusion, Don has learned to ask people to call back to our answering machine if they have a detailed message for me.

At times, Don misses nuances. Part of what brought us to counseling with a rehab psychologist several years ago came out of an incident when we were talking about the pressure I felt. We were focusing much of our lives on his recovery to the exclusion of other important things. I told Don, "I feel strain and pressure when you push hard all the time. I love you, but right now, the stress I am feeling has sapped away my *feelings* of love."

Don's eyes widened and he dropped his jaw in terror as he asked, "Are you leaving me?!"

"No. I'm not leaving you," I replied. "That's not what I mean. I still love you and I'm committed to you and to our marriage. But we have concentrated so much energy toward your recovery that we haven't taken time to enjoy each other or care for each other's emotional needs. Without that, I just don't *feel* very loving. I think all couples have times like that, even those who don't deal with brain injury."

I felt terrible when Don later told people, "Rosella doesn't love me anymore." There is a subtle difference between what I said and what he said, but he could not catch that nuance.

Don later said, "I was scared because I've heard terrible statistics of how many couples divorce after one of them has a brain injury." (Those statistics have since been challenged.) I reassured Don of my commitment to him, but he took a few weeks to settle down from that misunderstanding. He backed off some of the pressure he was putting on me, and more of my loving feelings toward Don returned.

Don occasionally asks a question that seems to me like something he pulled out of nowhere. In a conversation, his mind can move to a new subject, but he does not always verbalize the transition. Then he says a single word, without any explanation, followed by, "You know!" We fish around, and most of the time we find out what he means, but sometimes he says, "Oh, never mind."

Our conversations can become funny. One day I asked Don, "Is the Super Bowl in the afternoon or the evening this year?"

He said, "It's in the afternoon, but the pre-op is before that."

I do not know how to respond when Don says something like that. I don't want to laugh at him or make fun of him, even though what he says strikes me as funny. Occasionally I try to explain what he said, but he still does not understand. Every day we encounter mix-ups like this as we talk.

I tease Don when he frequently uses superlatives. He says, "That's the best meal I've ever eaten," or "That was the funniest movie I've ever seen." I think, *How can you eat the best meal or see the funniest movie of your whole life that often?*

Another example of Don's difficulty with language is the way he sorts dirty clothes into the baskets in our closet. Even though I have explained and demonstrated many times that he should put whites in one basket, colors in another, and dark clothes in the third, he still mixes things up. He understands the whites but sorts the rest by shirts and pants, rather than by colors. I have just given up on that one. But Don has made progress; now he can sort and fold our clothes after they are washed and dried. When he first came home from the hospital, he could not have successfully separated socks from underwear or physically folded them.

When Don is not being a huge tease, he is always polite to people. Many times he says, "Thank you for your kindness." He also says, "If you'd be so kind as to..." And he is forever saying, "Thanks much, yah." However, even though we have discussed this, he has a hard time inserting "please" in his requests to me. Don may say, "If you'll get me some water," or perhaps just, "Get me some water." I long for him to politely ask me for a favor instead of order me around. It seems easier for him to remember to say, "Thank you," than "Please."

Don used to say, "I'm no idiot," or, "Any idiot could figure out..." I felt bad when he said that. Even though I never called him an idiot, his comments seemed to suggest that he thought I had. But he was probably just expressing frustration. Don never used those expressions before his stroke; however, he was no longer his old self. I am relieved he has not used those "idiot" phrases for a long time.

Some TBI survivors completely lose their inhibitions and curse like they never did before their injury. Although Don's language was always clean and polite before his stroke, he says, "Since my stroke, the foul language I heard in the past at times floods into my mind when I get upset." When Don's agitation really flares, his paralyzed arm shakes and involuntarily contracts, his face turns red in an angry scowl, and out spurt some of those words between whatever else he has to say. Although this happens rarely, he says, "I feel bad after I curse and I don't want to do it. I always want to be polite."

Communication within our family

Don's inability to communicate effectively was probably the most devastating aftermath of his stroke, both for Don and for our family. The stroke changed the way he interacted with each of us. When we had confusing family discussions, I remember thinking that the boys and I were on the same page, but Don was in a different chapter. Don watched our boys naturally shift their questions away from him to me. We slipped into this pattern unintentionally as the boys and I became a lot more self-sufficient.

Don had a harder time initiating conversation on a deep level with our kids. He told me, "I'm frustrated that I can't talk to the boys like I used to." When he mixed things up, he sometimes said, "What I think doesn't even seem to matter anymore. I can't do anything right."

When Don felt bad, I felt bad. I tried to uphold his dignity and give him a voice in our decisions, but there were times when he entirely misunderstood the situation, and we all gave up in frustration. As time passed, Don's speech improved, and we all learned to roll more with the tide in tough situations.

We noticed another change in Don. He had usually interacted with us in a reasonable and gentle manner. But after his stroke, Don lost his emotional buffer and occasionally spoke to us in sharp tones. The boys and I at times drew back from those painful exchanges. Although we continued to love each other, many things changed in the way we related to each other. We all missed how life used to be.

One day I calmly said, "Don, there's some ketchup on your cheek."

He flared back, "Who cares?"

I wanted to say, "I care; I want you to look nice," but I hurt so much from his tone of voice that I shut down instead.

Usually Don is such a dear person, but little tense encounters sprinkled throughout a week continue to wear at us. It is hard to stop in the middle of a challenging interaction, recognize what is happening, step back, and initiate a more positive approach, especially when Don does not appear to be aware that he is speaking harshly or inaccurately.

We have both lost some of our former tolerance and patience in our reactions to each other. We sometimes find ourselves scared of each other, pulling back, guarding our words and behavior. At times I feel worn down and speak harshly. When I ask or say something Don thinks is critical, he may react sharply. I know I am overly sensitive and easily hurt, which makes him feel bad. We do a lot of hurting, apologizing, and forgiving. It is the only way we can continue to nurture our relationship.

Communication with Friends

I often hear Don miss points, misunderstand or confuse facts, or take unrelated tangents in conversations with people. We usually try to let his inaccuracies pass, but when he says, "I know I'm right," a wave of tension wells up in my chest. Other times if Don suspects he may be confusing people, he asks them, "Am I making sense?" Because people want to encourage him, they tend to say, "Yes," even if what he says does not totally make sense.

Don worked as a peer mentor for several years, visiting

other TBI survivors, whom his office called "consumers." He usually wrote down future appointments in his calendar when he visited the men, or I called them to make appointments for him. I always called the night before to confirm his meetings. However, when Don began his job, he wanted to make calls for himself. The first time he called one of his consumers, I heard Don say, "Hi. This is Don Kvernen. I'm a psychologist in town. Do you want an appointment?"

Moments later Don told me, "He said, 'No,' and hung up on me." Don could no longer present himself as a psychologist but did not seem to know what came out of his mouth. That whole encounter was a bust.

Another time Don called one of his consumers and said, "Hi, this is (the name of the man he called). I'm calling to confirm that I'll meet you at 3:30 at 507-(our phone number!)." Again, he seemed to have no idea that what he said was incorrect.

Although Don may be close to accurate in what he says, he is often off by several degrees. One day a friend asked Don, "How was your trip?" Don had a wonderful trip to North Dakota but answered instead by sharing details of the fun time he had at his birthday party. People are very kind. They graciously let those errors pass and keep on talking.

Prior to his stroke, Don loved to discuss ideas with people, but he can no longer participate in large group conversations like he did before. When Don says something in a group, he may digress to a slightly different topic. People at times have difficulty understanding what Don tries to tell them unless they ask him a number of questions. But even though Don can fail to follow what others say, many times he understands a conversation perfectly and makes quite insightful comments. He still loves to listen to people visit, but he says, "I feel sad and embarrassed by how I am. When I'm in a group, I just have to keep my mouth shut and listen."

Usually Don has to think so long before he says something that by the time he can speak, the conversation has moved on and he has lost his opportunity. He lifts his hand or opens his mouth but cannot quite jump into the conversation. When I notice those nonverbal signals, I try to ask Don what he is thinking to give him a chance to talk. He communicates one on one more easily than with a group.

Although Don seldom understands jokes, he picks up the spirit when people say something funny, and he laughs along with everyone. If I later ask, "Did you understand that joke?" he says, "No, I didn't get it." People are usually unaware of how much Don does not understand. His own sense of humor, however, is very much intact and quick.

I love how Don can turn language struggles into humor. One early fall evening, our friends sat with us at our table, and Don began to feel chilled. He said to Mike, "Would you close the...?" He pointed at the patio door and shook his finger as he searched for the word.

Mike said, "Door?"

Don responded, "Yeah." He shrugged his shoulders and joked, "That wasn't so hard." We all laughed.

A peculiar thing happens when we drive down the street in our neighborhood. Don waves at people but quits just before they see us. He also talks to people from inside our car when they cannot possibly hear or see him. He says, "Thanks for your kindness," or "Have a good day!"

When Don sees a friend, he may ask, "How is your mother doing?" I will have completely forgotten that our friend's brother had an accident; but, although Don does not say the facts accurately, he remembers. This happens regularly, and he finds great delight in telling people he recalls things better than I do. He is right.

After what I have described, it may not sound like Don has made much progress in language. But when we think back to how things used to be, we see huge strides. At first he could not read at all; now he can read to some extent. At first he could not use numbers at all; now he can, sometimes accurately. We used to stop in almost every conversation to decipher what he said, and this has improved. We are grateful for every bit of progress he has made. Over the years, friends have said, "Don, you are speaking much more clearly than when I saw you last year." Afterwards he says to me, "Wasn't that good to hear?"

What helps us cope and gives us hope:

- We keep asking Don questions until we think we understand what he wants to say.
- If we can catch the context, we ignore many of Don's mistakes with word usage.
- Don is basically a polite and kind person.
- Don tries not to use impolite language, even if it easily comes into his mind.
- I try to uphold Don's dignity and give him a voice in

our family discussions.

- When miscommunication hurts, we do a lot of apologizing and forgiving.
- When I notice Don is trying unsuccessfully to say something in a group, I create a break in the conversation and give him an opportunity to share his ideas.
- Don frequently turns his language struggles into humor.
- People encourage us when they tell Don how much he has improved from the last time they saw him.

Chapter 6
Receiving Help

Although Don had to work hard and learn to do many things for himself after his stroke, he could never have succeeded all on his own. He had to swallow his pride, humble himself, and accept help. Many people have supported him and helped him reach his current level of recovery.

Family's Help

Don often tells me, "I'm so grateful for you. You and the boys put up with me and loved me. I'm so glad you didn't leave me!" That is part of being a family—hanging together through challenging times.

Both Don's family and mine found countless ways to express their love for us. Family members helped with household tasks, offered advice when we asked, and even gave us financial gifts. They were always ready with an ear to listen or an encouraging word to give us hope. My sister Marlene carved out time to encourage me in our weekly phone chats.

When Jon graduated from high school, Don's brother Luther and his family offered to help with household repairs and preparation for Jon's party. Soon Don's mom and others decided to join them, and eventually ten of his family members descended on our house to work for an entire week. Neighbors let some of our relatives stay at their homes and became friends with them. If we had not accepted our family's offers of assistance or had not asked for help, we, our friends, and loved ones would have missed much.

After the Kvernen crew painted the exterior of our house in just one day, they proceeded to stain the deck the next day. But they did not stop there. They put edging and rock along one side of the house so the boys and I did not have to do as much trim work when we mowed. Luther repaired things and both the adults and kids worked incredibly hard. By the end of the week, I could not think of another thing to put on my to-do list. Don enjoyed the company and being together as much as getting the house repairs done.

One job on my list was to replace a damaged board on our deck. Luther casually listened to Don's instructions about where he had stored an extra board. He decided to search on his own, based on a general idea rather than Don's detailed instruction.

After Luther's first failed attempt, he returned and asked Don if he was sure he remembered where he had put the board. Again, Don gave precise directions, but Luther thought, *How could he remember where the board is when he can't even remember my name?*

After Luther's second failure to find the board, Don came out to the deck in his wheelchair. He kindly showed Luther that the board was exactly where he had said.

Luther later said, "At times we jump to conclusions about Don and give him less credit than he deserves. When we see how much has changed for Don, we tend to forget how much is still the same. We need to believe him."

Work—For a Sense of Independence and Value

Along with family, friends, and medical personnel, there are organizations that help people with brain injury (see Organizations and Resources). One of those in Rochester is the Southeastern Minnesota Center for Independent Living (SEMCIL), a nonprofit organization that assists people with disabilities to become independent and productive community members.[1]

Soon after Don left the hospital, he attended the SEMCIL Stroke Support Group. There he found other people who understood his struggles. He also participated in SEMCIL's Mild Traumatic Brain Injury Support Group where he found support from younger people. Each group helped him in slightly different ways. Eventually SEMCIL asked Don to co-facilitate the two support groups he attended. His job was to greet people and see that everyone had a chance to talk. SEMCIL offered workshops, home healthcare, a library, connections to resources, and a computer center where Don could try computer assistance programs.

Don told me, "I used to work hard and accomplished something by the end of the day. I wish I could find something to help me feel productive and give me value. I feel worthless just sitting around."

A speaker at a brain injury workshop resonated with us when he said, "Everyone needs something to do to make them feel worthwhile." However, because of Don's cognitive

---

1 http://www.semcil.org/about_us.html (accessed 1/28/2011)

scrambling, his paralysis, and his lack of stamina, neither the hospital nor community vocational rehab counselors could find any work Don could do.

After we exhausted our attempts to find any kind of work for Don, SEMCIL hired him as a peer mentor. Don qualified to be a peer mentor since he had experienced many of the same challenges his SEMCIL consumers had. He could no longer counsel professionally, but he could try to encourage other people who, like him, were survivors of brain injury or stroke. He usually met with his consumers once or twice a month. Because Don could not accurately confirm his appointments, I became his assistant and made those calls for him.

Ann Peterson, Don's boss, met with him to discuss any needs of his consumers and help Don with his records. She was extremely gifted in helping people. We believe the experience she had with her sister who survived a brain injury is part of what fed Ann's passion for her work.

Don joked about his pay at SEMCIL. "The first year I earned $5.50 an hour and only worked a few hours each week. In my former job I earned over $100 an hour. But even though I didn't earn much at SEMCIL, the opportunity to earn something was a big deal for me. During the years I worked as a peer mentor, I bought all our Christmas presents with the money I earned. That felt pretty good."

After working as a peer mentor for ten years, the regulations of the job increased so much that Don decided to quit. However, he continues his visits with the men he mentored on his own time. Most of these men can't get out much. They often tell him how much his friendship means to them. The men also mean a lot to Don. He loves visiting them. He tries to identify what each of them needs and see if he can provide it. For some it means listening, for others it means going out to eat.

Don says, "Without my job at SEMCIL, I would have gone crazy or probably suffered depression. The job gave me joy and satisfaction as well as new friends. I'm glad my SEMCIL job gave me some routine activity and purpose, and a bit of cash."

Don tells people, "When I hear people complain about their jobs, I think, *I'd give anything just to be working again.* If there was any way I could provide for myself and my family, I would. But I can't."

Disability Insurance

We buy insurance to carry us through unforeseen problems. Don and I do not want to exploit the system, but we feel Don's stroke was exactly the kind of thing for which we paid our premiums.

Don's stroke hit the core of his working ability—his mind. Because Mayo Clinic doctors diagnosed him as "totally and permanently disabled," Don was entitled to receive his private disability insurance income and Social Security Disability Income (SSDI). Social Security allows disabled people to earn a small amount, and he has never exceeded their limit. These two sources of income have kept us afloat financially.

Since Don cannot handle his finances, the Social Security Administration appointed me as his "Representative Payee." Social Security requires that once a year I submit a report to them varifying that we have spent Don's entire SSDI on him. I have to further divide his expenses between "Food and Housing" and

"Other." Because I need documentation for a potential audit, I spend time compiling a detailed report each month.

I wonder how older folks or people who cannot think clearly handle all the paperwork needed in situations like ours. If I was not so grateful for the income, the paperwork could take me over the edge.

No one thinks a disaster will happen to them, but Don is proof that insurance has made life incredibly easier after disaster struck. As a result of our experience, we highly recommend the purchase of health, disability, and life insurance.

Health Insurance

We also recommend you thoroughly check the terms of your insurance policies. Perhaps our experience can help you foresee and prevent what happened to us.

One day a woman from our health insurance company called me at home and said, "Mrs. Kvernen, is your husband working?"

I answered, "No, he's still in the hospital."

"Then we can no longer cover him with this health insurance policy," she said.

I was so taken by surprise that I could not think how to respond.

She explained that our health insurance was configured with Don heading the group as a self-employed person with our family members in the group under him. Since he could not work while he was in the hospital, Don no longer fit their criterion of being self-employed. We could not be covered even though we had paid all our premiums on time. We had assumed we bought health insurance to cover us if we became sick—No!

Due to our local insurance agent's fight for us, the company did not drop us at that point. They later tried again to terminate our coverage, but they eventually covered us until Don became eligible for Medicare and then dropped our whole family.

Waiver of Premium

Don had purchased the waiver of premium option on some of his life insurance policies. We paid a little extra each month for Don's premiums with the agreement that, if he became disabled, the company would waive his monthly payments but continue his coverage. For each insurance company that granted a waiver after Don's stroke, we signed annual requests to confirm he was still "totally and permanently disabled." They also required annual proof from Mayo Clinic of Don's continuing disability.

Another incident cemented our cynicism about insurance companies. The same company mentioned earlier terminated the waiver of premium on a small life insurance policy Don had that they had promised in writing to continue even after they terminated our health insurance. For years the statement on their request for proof of continuing disability had read, "This means you must be unable to do any type of work for which you are qualified by education, training, or experience, on even a part-time basis for pay or profit."

One year I noticed they had changed the wording. The new statement read, "Please advise if you are still permanently and totally disabled which makes you unable to work at any occupation."

When I called to make sure I was filling the form out properly, I told the insurance company about Don's SEMCIL job. They yanked the waiver of premium! Don's part-time job, for which he had been earning less than $150 a month, would cost our family $10,000 upon his death. Don had earned a PhD, so his peer mentor job at SEMCIL was hardly something for which he was "qualified by education." And he certainly did not consider his work an "occupation." We were frustrated for ourselves and upset that other disabled people, who wanted to work a small amount to regain their self-esteem, could be treated the same way.

Kreg Kauffman, an attorney on the SEMCIL board, presented our case to the Minnesota Department of Commerce. With the help of the Minnesota attorney general, our insurance company was fined on a number of violations of the state insurance code and was ordered to reinstate Don's waiver of premium, but they did not comply. After about three years, the company finally settled out of court and reinstated the waiver. However, no precedent was established that could help someone else in our position.

Meaningful Relationships

Friends have been a huge encouragement to Don since his stroke and have been a big part of what makes life meaningful to him. Don and I place a high priority on making and cultivating relationships with friends. Don says, "I hate to think where I'd be if I didn't have wonderful people in my life. I would much rather visit with friends than go to a movie or some other entertainment."

Not long after Don's stroke, we joined a new small group from our church. We listened to each other, cried together, celebrated together, and prayed for each other. We learned that our parenting concerns and other things that happened to us were common to the others as well. We felt more normal from having regular contact with these dear people. Years later, our care group continues to meet, and these folks remain some of our closest friends.

Our entire church family helped us raise our kids by modeling the faith and values that were important to us. They supported our family in tremendous ways. Shortly after Don's stroke, our church even had a special prayer service for our family and gave us a generous financial gift.

A benefit of living in Rochester has been to share our home with people who come to Mayo Clinic for healthcare. We have not kept track of the hundreds of nights people have stayed with us. Since Don's stroke, he finds special satisfaction in listening to and loving people who are going through crises. I take care of the hospitality, and we both care for our guests. Some start out as friends of friends but become like family to us. We find that we always receive more than we give.

Help with Computers and This Book

Early in Don's recovery, Bob Sinex, another retired IBM friend, helped Don with his reading practice. After a break of a few years, Bob returned to help Don again. Their time together evolved from reading practice to computers.

When Don first tried to use our home computer, he could

not make sense of the keyboard. He could copy a bit, but his brain could never compose while he was on the computer. It seemed that without a kinesthetic element, like Kay had used as she taught him to read, Don could not make connections in his brain to use the computer.

Don later wanted to try a voice recognition program at the SEMCIL computer center. Bob Sinex helped Don "train" the program to recognize his speech. Don needed to record extensive passages of reading material for the computer to recognize his words. However, because Don could not read well, Bob had to read phrases, and Don had to try to repeat them. That process was extremely difficult and laborious.

The voice recognition program works for people who say what they mean and who can recognize errors as they proofread. I knew from the beginning that Don could not accomplish either of these feats, but he was determined to try. So Bob and Don attempted to use the computer, but Don's cognitive problems did not allow him to understand the process.

For years Don talked about writing a book about his stroke, but he could not write without help. With his aphasia, Don had difficulty expressing the focus he wanted for the book, and I did not know how to tackle such a moving target. When Don told Bob about his desire to write a book, they gradually shifted their efforts in that direction. Bob took Don's wishes seriously and started the book for him.

With Bob's help, Don verbally entered some ideas onto SEMCIL's voice recognition computer program. Bob also took notes from many visits and transcribed what Don told him. However, because of Don's aphasia, I had to edit many of the details and chronology of what Bob wrote. Bob started the book, but over time I added other topics and details. I eventually became the primary author for the book.

These stories represent only a fraction of the help we have received over the past twenty years. Countless individuals, businesses, and organizations have supported us and walked with us through our struggles and losses. We are grateful.

What helped us cope and gave us hope:

- Family and friends found countless ways to express their love and care for us.
- When we saw how much had changed for Don, we needed to remember how much remained the same. We needed to believe in Don.
- Organizations and support groups provided resources and encouragement to Don and other people with disabilities.
- Although the search was difficult, when we finally found a job for Don to do, he felt much better about himself. It gave him routine activity and also some cash. Because Don could not manage his scheduling, I became his assistant.
- We had health insurance, disability insurance, and waiver of premium coverage with most of Don's life insurance. However, we should have read the fine print.
- There were good people to advocate for us and for other people with disabilities.

- We continued connections with old friends.
- Our faith and our church held all four of us together.

Chapter 7

Dealing with Losses

Don and other survivors of stroke or traumatic brain injury struggle with losses that are physical, mental, emotional, economic, and social. Although their brain injuries differ for each person, the effects often ripple into every area of their lives.

In addition to the losses our family experienced from Don's stroke, we suffered loss again in 2004 when our older son, Jon, died from cancer at the age of twenty-nine. Although we had eight precious months to make memories and say our goodbyes, the loss of a son we loved so much broke our hearts. Our tears and sobs are less frequent as time passes, but I am sure they will easily surface for the rest of our lives.

Two years before Jon died, I accepted a part-time job at our church. When I was working, Don spent quite a bit of time alone at home. He says, "I grieved deeply during the long winter after Jon died. I still think about Jon every day, but I especially struggle the weeks around the anniversary of his death."

Back in high school, Jon played Gershwin's *Rhapsody in Blue* on his trombone for a music contest. I almost burst with joy as I accompanied him on the piano. The first time I heard that piece after Jon died, I pulled over in my car and cried my heart out. *Rhapsody in Blue* still triggers my grief whenever I hear it. We are sad when we miss Jon, but we ease our pain by thinking of the good memories we have of him, how proud we are of him, and how blessed we were to have him for almost thirty years. I include more details in Chapter 11 about Jon's life and death.

Don says, "When I think of what I could do before my stroke and now cannot, I ache and feel empty sadness inside. I long for my former physical and mental abilities. I miss normal communication, relationships, and interactions with people. The losses I've experienced from my stroke cause me to feel grief, like something in me died."

Once when I (Rosella) felt sad over our losses, I thought of an image of sandcastles. We had a great time as we built elaborate sandcastles in the first forty years of our lives, but suddenly a wave came out of nowhere, demolishing them. As we gathered our senses to assess what remained of our former lives, little mounds of sand remained to prompt memories of what had been. Many intricate details that added meaning and joy to our lives had been swept away by the destructive wave of Don's stroke. So much was missing. After that, waves of grief followed.

Grief over our losses no longer dominates our lives. We moved on to predominantly good times, merely interspersed with down times. However, we have found it is therapeutic to talk about losses, especially with folks who have had similar experiences. We sense a bond with people when they say, "Yes, that's how I feel, too." We no longer feel alone in our situation. With that spirit in mind, we want to describe some of Don's losses.

Family Relations

At the time of Don's stroke, Jon was sixteen and Josh twelve years old. Even though Don survived his stroke and we still loved each other, we found ourselves in some ways with a new husband and father. We all missed how life used to be. Don said, "I ache when I remember how I used to relate to Rosella and the boys before my stroke and how our relationships have changed."

Before his stroke, Don loved to help with our kids' church activities. He coached soccer, went to the boys' games, and loved being a dad. We had a boat and went water-skiing, took the boys camping, and vacationed with them. All of this screeched to a halt after the stroke, except for Don's love for his kids.

Don could no longer lead our family as he had or carry out many of his former roles and responsibilities. When the boys and I had to pick them up, we had many tense encounters. We had to learn many new skills, like how to maintain the house, the boat, and the tractor. Since I had trouble finding Don's tools, I eventually rearranged them; but Don revealed his exasperation when he said, "She even messed with my garage."

That first fall, the boys and I needed to replace the mower on the lawn tractor with the snow blower attachment. Don tried to explain some of the steps to us, but we could not understand because of his aphasia. He also did not follow the sequence of the manual. I was irritated and confused until I realized we had to determine right and left as we faced forward on the tractor seat, rather than as we looked at the diagrams in the manual. We also did not understand many of the words in the manual. Our frustration escalated as we tried to figure out how to accomplish the task and still preserve Don's dignity. That incident made a bad memory for all of us.

Don tells me, "I'm proud of the way you picked up so many responsibilities, but I feel bad that you have to mow the lawn all the time and do such heavy work. I would give anything to take back some of my old jobs in our family."

We cope with the changes in our family relations by realizing we cannot go back to the way things used to be and by trying to accept our new reality. We can go on because we still love each other.

Work

Don always had a strong work ethic. I do not recall that he complained about any job he ever had. When he lost the counseling career that he loved, he missed the sense of accomplishment his work gave him and the satisfaction of providing for our family. Don has replaced this loss by becoming an encourager for many people.

Don says, "Before my stroke I enjoyed physical labor; we finished our basement, terraced our lawn, put in fencing, and built a storage shed. I liked to work at many of these projects by myself, but they were also fun family activities. I loved to mow the yard after a day of sitting in a chair and dealing with the stress in people's lives. After my stroke, I missed physical work as a hobby." We have not figured out a way to compensate for this loss.

Relationships in the Community

Don's stroke suddenly severed his associations with his clients, with colleagues, with professionals in the community, and with friends he made as they served together on committees. Although Don was still welcomed to his Rotary Club, he said he felt like he was in a fog as everyone rushed in from busy professional jobs and enjoyed intelligent conversations that he could not follow. Don also missed the friends he made at the drugstore, in his office building, at the grocery store, and at restaurants.

After some recovery, Don began to schedule lunch dates with his old friends or stop by their businesses to say hi. When I brought him to see those people, I noticed that his friends seemed as happy to see him as he was to see them. All had not changed.

Financial Freedom

We survived financially after Don's stroke. However, we missed our previous freedom to be less concerned about how we spend our money. We did not have to trim our clothing or food budget, but we significantly cut back on entertainment and vacations. Don loved to travel when he consulted in the States and overseas. Now he says, "I don't think I'll ever be able to physically handle a trip overseas again even if I could afford it."

When I watched travel agency commercials on TV shortly after Don's stroke, I felt sad because we would probably no longer visit those places. At the same time, I realized we had traveled more than many people and seen many sights I saw advertised. Still, tension existed between our loss and our good memories.

We coped with our new financial restrictions by remembering that we were happy at each of the varied levels of income during our early marriage. We had always tried to live within our means and go without if we did not have the money. That plan did not cause us to suffer in the past, and it has worked without much pain since Don's stroke. We are also glad we have many friends who are not materialistic.

Handling Finances

From early in our marriage, Don handled our financial matters. He was thorough and made good choices. When we discussed bigger money decisions, we rarely disagreed.

Don says, "When I had to turn everything over to Rosella, I missed taking care of our finances. As soon as I could go out on my own, I learned to pay for my own purchases or for my lunch and a tip. I chose to give cashiers more money than I thought was needed and then ask if I gave them enough. I had to trust they gave me the correct change. Later I learned to use my credit card. Spending money independently helped me regain some dignity."

About fifteen years after his stroke, Don learned to write a check to get cash from his checking account. I printed a mock $200 check that he could copy and take to the bank. He said, "I'm so glad I can go out on my own and not have to ask for money or depend on someone else to pay for me."

We have always had enough. God has always provided for us above what we have needed. We put two sons through college, replaced vehicles, sold our home ourselves, and bought another. I learned how to figure out taxes and how to understand six different medical insurance plans for various family members. I enjoy keeping records organized, but I sometimes become frustrated, trying to understand details or fighting with my computer. Don wishes he could handle our finances, but he tells me, "I'm proud of how you picked up our money matters."

Mobility

Don recovered partially from the loss of his ability to walk. However, he is still limited in how far and under what conditions he can walk. At times he stays home or sits in the car because he is not mobile enough to join me.

One day shortly after his stroke, I sat at a café across the street from Saint Marys Hospital. Glancing out the window, I noticed men in neat business suits, walking hurriedly by on the sidewalk outside. Tears came to my eyes as I thought, *Those men are completely oblivious of how blessed they are to be able to walk. I wonder if Don will ever walk like that again.*

Don coped with his loss of mobility by working very hard in PT and by exercising. He also learned to accept the need for his wheelchair when we traveled and to use a scooter in a large store or at a fair or theme park. Even though Don is limited, he still gets around and has fun.

Independence

Don intensely grieved his loss of independence when he could not drive. It seemed to him that he could not do anything on his own. Don hated to make me take him everywhere he went, and he longed to be independent. Not much time passed before he started to dream of driving again. I tell about how he accomplished that in Chapter 9.

Self Sufficiency

Don cannot do many things for himself since his stroke. I have to cut his fingernails and toenails. He can microwave leftovers but cannot cook for himself. It is difficult for him to cut his meat even with a rocker knife. Because he cannot do housework or maintenance, he has to depend on others to help him.

Since gas pumps are not standardized, they present a challenge to Don. He has trouble reading the choices or pressing the right buttons, so he usually asks another customer or a station employee to help him. Otherwise I fill his van with gas for him. When Don orders food at a restaurant, he does not always get what he thinks he ordered. He wishes he could do more for himself, but he has learned to ask for help when he has troubles.

Spontaneity

Don's stroke stole much of his freedom to be spontaneous and to make choices on his own. One day a friend asked Don to take him to buy a used car he had seen advertised in the newspaper. Neither of them knew where they were going. They first ended up in Lake City, thirteen miles up-river from their target, but they eventually reached their destination. Don's friend liked the car and bought it.

I came home from work that day and did not find Don, so I called him on his cell phone. When he answered, he said, "I'm in La Crosse!" [Wisconsin]

As I recovered from the shock that Don had not told me about his seventy-mile road trip, his friend corrected him from the background, "No, we're in Wabasha." That was only forty miles away.

"We're ready to leave for home. I'll tell you all about our trip when I come home."

I could hear excitement in his voice. (I was having other thoughts myself!)

Don later told me that he led their return, even though he did not know which road to take. Part way home, they stopped and concluded that neither of them knew where they were. But Don knew they would find Rochester if they hit either of two four-lane roads—the Interstate on the south of them or Highway 52 on the west. They drove the curvy back roads up from the Mississippi and eventually reached home after dark.

Don had not enjoyed such spontaneous fun or felt such accomplishment since before his stroke. All on their own, the two friends had successfully completed a road trip of about a hundred miles! When Don walked into the house that night, he could hardly contain his glee. I had really worried about him, but he was so ecstatic I resisted my urge to scold him and let him enjoy the tales of his adventure. Don needs opportunities for spontaneity.

Making Plans

In contrast to our desire for spontaneity, we have to keep

our plans tentative. Don may suddenly not feel up to doing whatever we have arranged. There are times we cancel an activity at the last minute, or I go by myself. That unpredictability can be quite frustrating for both Don and me.

Once after we became empty nesters, Don and I made vacation plans to travel to Ontario to visit friends. We were excited, anticipating fun with them and a break from my job. But at the last minute, after I had made our travel arrangements and scheduled my time off work, we had to cancel because Don's back had terrible spasms. We cope best if we keep flexible and do not allow changes to frustrate us.

Dignity

Don sometimes struggles with his loss of dignity. He becomes frustrated when I ask him to do something that used to be completely his own choice. Because of his irritable bladder, there are times when he suddenly has to go to the bathroom. I think he might be wise to go to the bathroom before we go into a movie or concert, but he often does not want to go.

When our kids were young, we made them go to the bathroom if we knew there would not be a chance later, even though they did not feel a need to go. I do not always ask Don if he needs to stop at a restroom, but if I do, I try to be discrete. Yet Don occasionally responds, "No. If I don't have to go, I don't have to go!"

I wonder, *What if he has to go to the restroom before the intermission and can't navigate the stairs in the dark? What if he waits until intermission and he can't make his way through the rush for the restrooms?* I feel frustrated that I do not dare ask Don about this, and he feels humiliated if I do ask him. I need to be careful to protect Don's dignity.

Singing

Don had a nice voice and loved to sing from the time he was young. His family used to hear him sing from across the fields when he drove the tractor. He sang in college and church choirs and also sang solos.

After his stroke, Don could no longer maintain good breath support, and his pitch became wavering. Instead of the strong baritone voice he used to have, his voice was weak. He missed singing and interacting with choir friends, as well as enjoying music for a hobby. About fourteen years after his stroke, Don started singing in church choir again. Since he had difficulty reading the music and words, he learned primarily by repetition and by listening to the men next to him. He enjoyed choir and thought his voice grew stronger, but he quit because the climb up the steps to the choir loft was too difficult. Don still sings along with others, but he no longer sings solos.

Keeping up with Others

Don's stroke slowed him down to a crawl; he fell out of step with the world around him. His previous responsibilities kept him busy, maybe too busy. Now he feels like he is in the slow lane. Everyone else speeds by him, and he misses being able to keep up with them. In a heartbeat, Don would trade his times of boredom for a little of the anxiety and stress that come with an active life. We no longer can keep up with others, so we enjoy what we can and look for people and activities in the slower lane of life.

Loss of Previous Goals

Since Don's stroke, both of us have sensed an emotional vacuum that is hard to explain. Although our lives are meaningful in many ways, when we look at other people, we imagine they all have goals, plans in their lives, and things they are looking forward to doing. That's not the way our lives are anymore. We have changed much from our happy-go-lucky twenties and thirties.

On the other hand, much of what we see people strive after seems shallow to us, and we sense a far deeper fulfillment from our perspective. However at times, Don and I feel out of sync with the world because we do not fit in as well as we used to.

We have heard other people our age express similar feelings, so this may have something to do with our age and empty nest. However, we did not slip gradually into these feelings; they began abruptly at the time of Don's stroke. Many of our previous goals and dreams suddenly went down the drain. We have learned we have to let go of some of our former dreams and dream new, more realistic ones that work for our new circumstances.

Don does not feel intense grief for his losses all the time, but there certainly are times when he gets down or discouraged. We do not mean to complain about our losses. Rather, we want to share them with you to help you not feel alone with your losses. If you have friends or family with brain injury, you may better understand what life can be like for them. This is what our life is like; we are proud of some of our adjustments and embarrassed by others.

What helps us cope and gives us hope:

Don has consciously decided not to dwell on his losses, because those thoughts could suck him into a deep emotional hole. Instead, we both try to think about what we do have; and really, that list is long.

Don, Rosella, Jon, and Josh before Don's stroke. December 1989
Photo by Jacobson Studios, Mayville, ND

Don in PT gym. Note his asymmetrical face. April 1991

Don with his reading tutor Kay Hawley. Note his tray of rice. 1992

Family picture taken shortly before Jon's cancer was discovered. August 2003

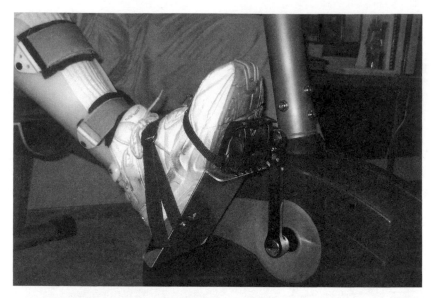

Platform pedal for exercise bike. 2010

Don ready to drive his van. 2010

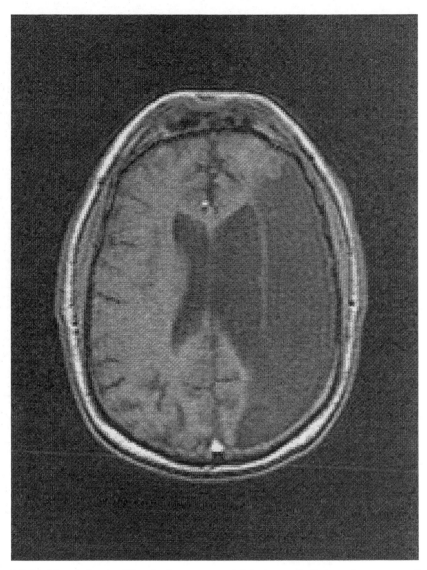

MRI of Don's brain. The dark portion of this image indicates the extent of Don's stroke. This view appears as if seen from Don's feet. The right side of the image shows the left side of his brain, which controls movement on the opposite, right side of his body. Don's body reabsorbed the dead tissue after his stroke, and spinal fluid replaced that space on the left side of his brain. November 2009

Chapter 8
We Needed Counseling

Not long into Don's recovery, his doctor encouraged each of us in our family to meet with a psychologist or psychiatrist. Dr. Lie said, "All of you have gone through huge changes in your lives. I think you could benefit by talking about your adjustments with a counselor."

Don thought he was adapting pretty well and did not need counseling. However, he did as he was told, and after one visit he said, "Good enough." The boys and I went to varied amounts of counseling. We moved on, thinking we were coping the best we could.

Several years later, Don and I realized we needed counseling again to help us resolve some of our tension. We made an appointment with one of the psychologists Don had come to know during his outpatient rehab.

Tension about Getting Back to Work

One reason we went to visit Dr. Smigielski was that Don was consumed by his efforts to get back to work as a psychologist. This caused stress for me because I did not see evidence that he was capable of returning to his job.

Early in Don's recovery, he had expressed confidence that he would eventually work again. In their love for Don, no one wanted to pop his bubble and tell him the time had come to shut down his practice. I knew, but for months I went along with him. Whenever the idea surfaced, Don insisted, "We can't shut down my practice. If I do that, I'll lose hope. We need to keep paying the rent." I saw that his hope was therapeutic for him, but maintaining his hope came at a significant financial cost and created emotional tension for me.

We had spent a lot of time and energy, as well as money, to help Don improve. Unable to bear the idea of losing his license to practice psychology, he attended classes to keep up his continuing education credits. In spite of inner reservations, I took him to seminars and complied with his requests to fill out his attendance forms. I felt very uncomfortable in that position. We also kept paying Don's license fees to keep the possibility open for him to return to work. Although Don thought this plan was working, I had my doubts; I could not talk with him because he did not want to even mention the subject.

A couple years after Don's stroke, he told people he was making great progress and was hoping to return to work by the end of the year. People rejoiced at this possibility, saying they were also convinced he would work again. I did not want to challenge them, but I wrestled within myself over the contradiction between what I saw and what others said. No one knew for certain what Don's future held. I wanted to support Don and did not want to dash his hopes, but I felt quite alone in recognizing Don's limitations. When I listened to what I thought were unrealistic predictions, my chest tightened with stress.

At our first visit with Dr. Smigielski, I told him, "We need an objective assessment of how much recovery Don has made since his stroke, so we can more accurately determine if he will ever be able to work again as a psychologist. We need help to come to terms with the differences in how we see this."

Don asked, "Can you tell me the criteria for me to work again? Could we arrange for an experience to observe the level of my counseling skills?"

As we talked further with our psychologist, I said, "I think we are a long way from Don returning to work. Can you help us identify some intermediate goals we can aim for on the way to Don's long-term goal of returning to his practice?"

Dr. Smigielski asked Don, "What skills do you hope to regain between now and the end of the year that would allow you to return to work as a psychologist?"

Don answered, "I would have to be tested and arrange supervision to observe my counseling abilities."

Dr. Smigielski explained, "Don, you just answered what you would have *to do*, rather than answering my question about what skills you need *to regain*. The tool you worked with as a psychologist was your mind. You were well trained and good at what you did. But your stroke damaged your mind—your tool. If you return to work, you need to sense nuances and understand complex situations. After losing abilities in areas of communication, you might recover to normal; but to work as a psychologist, you need to recover your communication skills to above normal."

Dr. Smigielski gently tried to help Don understand, if not fully accept, reality. He continued, "I think it is in the realm of very, very unlikely that you will ever return to work as a psychologist."

He suggested, "Don, you can take a battery of tests that will show not only your weaknesses but also your strengths. You can then build on your strengths."

But Don replied, "I know I'm not ready, so there is no point to pursue the testing yet."

Although this reality check was a huge blow to Don, Dr. Smigielski's assessment created a turning point as we dealt with the pressure we felt as a couple. Don felt deflated when he learned he probably would never work again. He continued to hold onto hope, even though he knew in his head that Dr. Smigielski was right. After Don heard it was very, very unlikely he would return to work, he told people he had a two to five percent chance. He could not give up completely. After Dr. Smigielski confirmed what I thought, I sensed less stress when those situations arose. I still did not contradict people, but I no longer had to doubt or question my instincts.

Overcome With Recovery

One day when we met with Dr. Smigielski, he said, "Try this idea on for size and see if it fits. Don, you've lost everything with your stroke: You can no longer work, no longer communicate the way you used to, no longer take care of your family, no longer do almost everything you used to do. Rosella has had to pick up everything that you can no longer do. Is that the cause of your frustration? Or could the problem be that you, Rosella, and your boys all lost everything, and that recovery has taken over your lives?"

This statement opened new understanding for us. We did not realize we had slipped into a pattern of focusing the predominance of our energies on Don's recovery. Don wanted to get back to the way life used to be, to return to work as a psychologist, to drive, to learn to read, to regain all the abilities he had lost. Medical people predicted that functions not restored within the early weeks and months after a stroke probably would not return. Don wanted to prove them wrong. With that goal, he worked for hours each day at physical exercises and at reading exercises.

Becoming engrossed by rehab, we forgot to enjoy life in the present. In the beginning, I shut down my personal activities and projects without hesitation in order to concentrate on Don's recovery. There are adjustments one makes automatically in a crisis. Neither of us thought much about what I gave up of my own time and interests. However, when the crises eased, we kept up the same patterns and pace, creating unrecognized stress.

One day Dr. Smigielski asked me what kinds of activities I enjoyed. As I contemplated an answer, tears welled in my eyes and my voice choked. The shock of my sudden, strong emotions made me realize that we had been doing what Don wanted so much that I could no longer even identify what I enjoyed.

In retrospect, I had cut back to only one scheduled activity per week for myself. Everything else was either for the boys or especially for Don. Don's quest to recover and relearn had taken a higher priority than just *being*. To me, it appeared that rehab had become more important for Don than anything, at times even more important than the boys and me and other relationships.

While I am sure I was doing some things I liked, we were

certainly on a pendulum swing. Our relationship grew healthier as we swung back to more intentionally search for what I liked and what we both liked to do.

Without realizing, we had slipped into many poor patterns. While the boys were in high school, Don and I used one car and the kids the other. About the time Josh went off to college, our second car died. I thought we could wait until the following spring to buy another car. That would help us financially and also keep me from worrying about Don driving on the ice in the winter.

One night, Don told his friends at his brain injury support group about his frustration. He wanted independence and wanted his own car. When I picked Don up, one of the guys rolled over to me and announced, "The group voted unanimously that you should buy a car for Don."

Don felt restricted and frustrated, but I also felt pressure from many directions. Without realizing what I was doing, I compensated by cutting back on doing things for myself in order for our car to always be available whenever Don wanted to go somewhere.

Here too, Dr. Smigielski helped us see our situation more clearly. As we talked this through, I felt new permission to reorganize my life around some of the desires I had suppressed for a long time and yet continue to help Don. Once in a while, I also just needed to be alone.

Leisure

At another of our counseling sessions, our psychologist asked us to write a list of leisure activities we both enjoyed.

Although there were things we could do with other people, we needed to look for recreation that was satisfying to both of us because of the well-being and intimacy it promoted in our marriage. When we failed to complete the task by our next appointment, we realized this was not a high priority for us.

Don's limitations curtail many of our former recreation options, so we struggle to find new ideas. However, we do have fun together. I read books aloud to Don, or we look at old pictures together. We take a drive in the country or go out for a Coke and talk, which gives me more pleasure than going out for dinner. Our piano brings joy to both of us; I love to play and Don loves to listen. After years of picking disappointing videos, we tried Netflix and found that their rating feature has finally helped us choose good movies. We also appreciate the entertainment public radio and public television provide for us.

We enjoy having friends come to our home for a meal or to stay with us. However, once Don invited a few of his SEMCIL consumers over for dinner, and I found less pleasure in the event than he did. I had to clean the house, make multiple trips around town to give rides for our guests, help those who were in wheelchairs get in and out of our house, and make a meal timed with all that. Even Don realized we should not repeat a party with that many moving parts.

Don and I like to travel, but he often gets anxious, and he tends to rush to arrive somewhere and later rush home. This can take the zip out of a trip for me. I like to relax and enjoy the travel itself. Don has improved in recent years, but he still needs to be twenty minutes early. At times when I grab my coat to leave the house, I find that, even in the winter, he is already waiting for me out in the car.

Decision-making Patterns

We talked in counseling about how we had lost our pre-stroke balance in making decisions as a couple. Don now had such limited choices in everyday life. He felt he depended on me or complied with my wishes all the time. We still shared in some decision making and worked well together. However, Don thought I sometimes took charge without consulting him. Occasionally he wanted me to decide matters. Other times he wanted to take part in the decision-making process but could not because he did not understand the situation.

I struggled with knowing when I should let go and let Don make choices. There were situations in which I might have to bear the brunt of the consequences if things did not go well. If he had an accident and hurt himself or others, I would have to care for him and pick up the pieces.

Offer Choices

Dr. Smigielski suggested, "Rosella, you can perhaps try to offer Don more choices and draw him into everyday decisions. Whenever possible, if you give him alternatives, you will help Don maintain his sense of self-worth and independence. When you disagree on decisions, look for Plan B rather than have either of you 'win' or 'lose' Plan A. Then the two of you will feel on the same side of the issue. That helps both of you feel better about a decision and eliminates a situation in which you give or deny permission for Don to do something. You also need to help Don retain his power to say, 'No.'"

Disregard More of Don's Errors with Numbers

Don regularly quoted numbers incorrectly. He told people he was eighty-three years old when he was really in his forties, or he said he used to make over $10 an hour when he made over $100 an hour. Dr. Smigielski suggested that I let more of Don's errors with numbers just pass rather than frequently correct him; this would cause him less embarrassment. I tried to follow that advice, but every incident required a decision on my part. *Should I or shouldn't I correct him this time?* I struggled with this issue more when we were with people we did not know than with friends who understood Don's condition.

Irritations

I am quite ashamed to admit that I allow Don's words and actions to irritate me so often. Some of these frustrations involve food. Don frequently talks about his need to lose weight. On our way to a restaurant, he sometimes says he is going to eat light. However, moments later he tells me, "I'm really hungry. I think I'll take a full-size meal with fries." He also cannot seem to understand which are high or low caloric choices when we talk about items on a restaurant menu.

During dinner one night, I asked Don if he wanted some vegetables. He said, "No, thanks. I'll just have a piece of pie instead." He may refuse healthy food and in the next breath ask for two of his frozen tofu dessert sandwiches. Before his stroke, Don would have handled those situations with a little more finesse. He would have eaten at least a little of his vegetables before he asked for dessert. My irritation probably stems from my childhood when I did not get dessert unless I ate my vegetables.

Don cannot figure out how to keep his head up and put food straight into his mouth. Instead he leans his face down toward the food and brings it up into his mouth. This is also true with liquids. His coordination and understanding limit him. Because Don usually draws in his breath when he takes a bite, he tends to choke on his food. He routinely holds his spoon or fork between his thumb and forefinger rather than between his thumb and first two fingers; that does not give him much control.

Since Don has little sensation on his right side, he asks me to tell him when I see food around his mouth, but he gets frustrated when I do. He tries hard to "do things right," so my comments probably accentuate what he perceives as his shortcomings. Even though I know I should let these minor annoyances go, I wish we could calmly inform each other of broccoli in our teeth or the like, graciously thank each other, and avoid becoming aggravated.

I feel embarrassed that I allow other little things that Don does to irritate me. Early on after his stroke, he faced the other people when he entered elevators instead of facing the doors. That felt really weird and uncomfortable for me. He likes to walk along the left side of a hall and keep his hand with the cane next to the wall, ready to help him in case he loses his balance. His therapists say that is typical of people like Don. However, I feel quite awkward when I walk with Don against traffic. He usually walks where he chooses, but I like to move to the right.

Tolerate or Talk out Irritations — Don't Stuff Them

We talked with our psychologist about how I handle my feelings when Don's actions irritate me. He is afraid of making mistakes that he knows annoy me, but he often does exactly what he tries so hard not to do. I do not want to badger him about these behaviors, and I try to tolerate frustrations and let those feelings go; but when I have a hard time suppressing my irritation, I either say something or I withdraw.

We decided that I should try to be tolerant, but that I should tell Don how I feel, rather than stuff my frustration. We also concluded that Don should work at what he knows pleases me and try not to react in anger if I point out a failure to him.

I have to confess that I cope with some of the eating irritations by turning on the news at mealtime. When the TV distracts me, my feelings of frustration do not as easily escalate to the level that I cannot control them. This is not a very healthy coping mechanism, but it eases my aggravation.

Better Communication

We struggled to improve our communication. I hurt a lot because I kept so much inside and was scared to tell Don my thoughts since he occasionally responded to what I said with frustration in his voice. At times he kept things inside, too. I did not know where to draw the line; should I confront him or let matters go? We did not want to hurt each other, but we did.

In my effort not to hurt Don, I sometimes beat around the bush when I talked with him. Dr. Smigielski encouraged me not to talk in circles because I probably confused Don. I should simply cut to the point, even if it hurt. It is hard to tell how successful I have been at this.

Looking for Tasks for Don

At the time we went to counseling, I carried out most of the tasks needed in our lives. Dr. Smigielski suggested we look harder for what Don could do. He began to fold clothes, empty the dishwasher, open and close blinds, and lock the doors at night. Don says, "I didn't like doing those things at first, but I realized they helped Rosella, and she probably didn't like doing them any more than I did." These days when I see that Don has emptied the dishwasher, I tell him how much I appreciate his help. His contributions toward our household tasks show me he cares.

Don's Self-Esteem

Don talked about how he felt ashamed when he messed up his speech. Dr. Smigielski said, "Don, if you base your self-esteem on your performance in language and accuracy, you are doomed to failure. In many ways your identity has shifted. However, Rosella can't make you feel adequate. Your feelings of adequacy can only come from within you."

Don knew that concept but needed a reminder. This advice also absolved me from the responsibility I had assumed to make Don feel good about himself.

Helpful Counsel

Counseling helped us at that point in Don's recovery. As

a wise third party, our psychologist gave us good advice and helped us out of some ruts in which we were stuck.

Determination and diligence are good and necessary for recovery. If Don had not been so determined, even though he was unrealistic at times, he would not have made as much progress as he has. Someone once said, "If you never shoot for the moon, you will never reach the roof." On the other hand, we needed to be reminded that there is still life to live even while Don tries to recover and conquer his challenges.

How Don chooses to live life greatly affects him and those around him whom he loves. How I interact and react with Don has a great effect on his well-being. We are still striving to keep that elusive balance between recovery and life. Professional advice helped us when we slipped out of balance.

What helped us cope and gave us hope:

- We sought counseling when we needed help.
- When we wanted to know if Don could go back to work, we asked a professional.
- When we realized that recovery had taken over our lives, we tried harder to balance life and recovery, to appreciate the present and enjoy each other more.
- We discovered our focus was predominantly on Don, so we looked for more activities we both enjoyed.
- I tried to give Don more choices and give him the option to say, "No."
- When Don made language errors, I learned to let more of them go uncorrected.

- I tried to tolerate or talk with Don about my irritations and not stuff them.
- Instead of talking in circles and confusing Don, I learned to cut to the point, even if it hurt.
- We looked more seriously for tasks Don could do around the house.

Chapter 9
Tackling Challenges

Stroke recovery is an unrelenting challenge. Any of the progress Don has made occurred over an extended period of time after strenuous work. But even though he has worked hard for many years, Don's determination did not guarantee results.

When people say, "I won't allow this illness to defeat me," their comments strike me as somewhat naïve and insensitive. Don's incomplete stroke recovery and our son's death from cancer did not happen from a lack of willpower. I like our friend's comment better; he said after his cancer diagnosis, "I'm going to live until I die." We cannot control everything that happens to us, but we can enjoy life as it is and tackle the challenges we face.

Don struggles to resolve his problems, taking much more time and energy than the average person needs. He strains to perform activities of daily life like dressing, eating, and understanding what people say. He fights barriers in his mobility and hits limits to his stamina. His restrictions curb his independence. And yet he is determined to go on. Throughout the years, Don has said, "I don't want to sit back and let my life deteriorate. I want to keep working to improve."

In many cases, Don can learn and improve. Other times he simply needs to learn to compensate. Now that he is sixty years old, his slow upward slope of improvement seems to be intersecting with the downward slope of aging. But even though life has its challenges, he does not want to give up.

Beyond Don's adjustment to his many losses, he has faced challenges with seizures, medications, exercise, learning to drive, safety, finding adaptive devices, and discovering ways to compensate. The list is long.

Seizures and Medications

Throughout Don's rehab, we were deluged with overwhelming amounts of information. We listened to more than we could absorb; some facts did not sink in. For example, we do not remember hearing that seizures are a potential danger after a stroke.

Nine months after Don's stroke, our family drove to North Dakota to celebrate Christmas with Don's extended family. One night the whole gang—Grandma, Don's siblings and their spouses, and all the nieces and nephews—went out to our favorite pizza shop for dinner. Before Don could enjoy much of his pizza, he began to shake violently and for several minutes could not respond to us. This first seizure scared and upset our entire family and everyone in the restaurant!

Someone called for an ambulance, which took Don to the nearby hospital. The hospital staff gave him his first anti-seizure medication and talked of airlifting him to Fargo. However, because of snowy weather, they instead sent him by ambulance about sixty miles to the larger hospital. Partway along his ride to Fargo, the fog in Don's mind lifted. For the rest of the ride, he visited and joked with a friend from high school who worked as an EMT in the ambulance.

When he arrived in Fargo, the Merit Care Hospital staff examined Don in the ER. Back at the pizza shop, I had at first wondered if Don was dying. I was shocked when they sent him home with me that night. I was afraid he might have another seizure. But he did not have another one on our trip, and we returned home to the Mayo Clinic to begin the search for a medication that would control his seizures.

Dilantin (phenytoin) was the first *anticonvulsant* Mayo doctors prescribed for Don, but within a month he experienced another generalized seizure. He had several seizures before they found the right medication that was effective for him. I happened to be with Don each time he had a seizure. He always sensed a *pre-seizure aura*, the brief feeling that a seizure was coming, and had a second or two to say, "I'm having a seizure!" He experienced a generalized seizure in the car while riding home from Rochester, some while lying on our bed, and one big one while he was riding our exercise bicycle.

In order for Don to exercise, I bound his paralyzed foot to the pedal of our Schwinn Airdyne bike with an ACE bandage. One morning I was sitting about two feet away from him at my desk, as I always did in case he needed help. When he realized a seizure was coming, I barely had time to jump up and grab him before it started. That time I watched the clock for eight long minutes, wondering if the seizure would ever end. Since Don is a heavy man, I had to hang on tightly to keep him from falling off the bike. He shook so uncontrollably I could not even move to improve my grip on him.

His doctor changed Don's anticonvulsant medication to

Tegretol (carbamazepine), but ultimately that did not work for him either. Don had a seizure about every four weeks. Finally, the anticonvulsant Depakote (divalproex sodium) proved effective to keep Don seizure-free.

Some of Don's meds had adverse side effects. When he took Depakote, he felt famished whenever he was awake. After he finished a meal, he wanted to eat it all over again. Don usually woke up at 7:00 a.m. to take his meds. Although he often wanted to sleep more, Don's hunger made him get up and eat breakfast before he went back to bed. For several years his weight crept up by at least five pounds a year. Finally Don's doctor said, "There's no way you can beat this weight problem. We need to try another medication for your seizures."

Dr. Rohren prescribed Keppra (levetiracetam) that for years has successfully controlled Don's seizures. Even though he was seizure-free before the medication change, he had to experience six months without seizures before he could drive again. Don has had no seizures while on Keppra. He is very relieved to no longer feel constantly hungry.

A few years after his stroke, Don began to experience incidents of a sudden urgency to urinate. He had to fight to control himself while he also concentrated on his walking, but he could not do much of anything quickly. A number of times Don lost the battle. Some of those occasions were private and frustrating, but a few were public and humiliating for him and for our family. Dr. Rohren prescribed Detrol for Don, which solved this problem and helped Don both physically and emotionally.

Because Don cannot forget the panic he used to feel and

worries he may have to suddenly go to the bathroom, he usually asks me to park up close to the building in a handicapped parking spot when I have to run an errand. His handicapped parking sticker helps him in many ways.

Exercise

Exercise is important but is also a challenge for Don. When he first went home, Don walked with help on our fifty-foot driveway. When he had mastered and become bored with the driveway, he decided to walk at our grocery store. He became exhausted the first time he walked to the back and returned to the front again. But after a while, he added multiple aisles to his grocery store routine. The next exercise phase involved the Schwinn Airdyne. But after his seizure on the bike, Don decided he never wanted to sit on top of that again, so we bought a lower, recumbent bike. When he became bored with that, we also sold the recumbent bike.

About that time, a new athletic club opened a great facility in Rochester. We purchased a family membership, and Don thrived on the social aspect of exercising at the club. At first he walked with his cane around the track, always trying to increase his distance.

After he grew bored with walking, Don wanted to try swimming. I cut a foam pool noodle into two lengths and rigged straps and clips to float his paralyzed arm. Three times a week, he dog-paddled up and down a swim lane for thirty to forty-five minutes. When Don swam, I wanted to be with him in case he had trouble in the water. I also needed to accompany him across the slippery floor and help him dress in the family changing rooms. He always felt invigorated after swimming. We continued the swimming routine for a few years.

When we moved into Rochester, Don decided to quit swimming and save money by walking on our neighborhood sidewalks. When winter came, he drove to Target and pushed a shopping cart around the store. He could talk to more people that way. During the summer, he progressed to pushing a grocery cart twice all the way around the outside of the huge Super Target complex.

When Don began to encounter repeated episodes of severe back spasms, his doctor suggested, "Don, your asymmetric walk puts a lot of stress on your back. Perhaps you should try another form of exercise and see if that eases your back pain." The doctor also prescribed some stretches and exercises to strengthen Don's back.

We bought another recumbent bike and put it in the room Don used for an office. I bought a racing pedal and hired a sheet-metal worker to make a platform that I screwed onto it. This time we wired the room for cable TV, which helps him stay on task as he exercises. Each morning I strap Don's right foot onto the platform, set the bike's program for him, and turn on the news. When he is feeling well, he tries to ride the bike for twenty minutes, five days a week.

Don feels better when he exercises, and his whole body works better. He is glad he has developed a routine for aerobic exercise that no longer hurts his back. Don's muscles become sore and he gets so tired he often has to go back to bed, but he does not like to miss the benefits of exercise.

Driving

Learning to drive was another challenging experience. At first, Don was completely incapable of operating a vehicle. After he developed seizures, he had to remain seizure-free for a year before he could consider getting behind the wheel of a car. As his recovery progressed and his seizures were brought under control, he began to long for the freedom to drive again.

Don first focused on his garden tractor. The autumn before his stroke, we bought a beautiful, new John Deere 318 tractor, which he hardly used before his stroke. During his recovery, Don had to watch our teenage children and me break in the tractor. He grew up in a family who thought John Deere was the best brand of implement, and he struggled with his inability to operate his new tractor.

Don thought that, if he could not drive a car, maybe he could at least handle the tractor. I saw things differently than he did. I worried about Don, but he was persistent.

For several reasons, I did not have confidence that Don was capable of driving. He could not demonstrate the difference between "fast" and "slow." He confused opposites. The hand controls of our tractor were located on the right side of the steering column. This meant that in addition to steering, he had to shift gears and accelerate with only his left hand, reaching across to the opposite side. Besides that, we had a treacherous lawn; he needed to navigate around trees on a steep hill, avoid a retaining wall and a barbed wire fence at the bottom edge, and steer clear of branches that dragged over the tractor in places. However, Don was determined to try.

We talked with an occupational therapist who said their

department had a battery of tests to check driver readiness skills. Usually they did not allow the spouse to observe. But because Don was taking the test just to see if he could operate a tractor, not a car, they let me watch.

There were many parts to the test: reaction time, vision, and side vision...and Don performed well at everything! After the exam, I gave up resisting and let him try the tractor. The first time back on his tractor, I hung on behind Don while he mowed a flat part of our yard by our driveway. Some of his driving skills seemed to return automatically. As he improved, he gradually mowed more and more.

One day Don misjudged the edge of a small strip of lawn that ran alongside our deck. The grass was a little wet, and he went a little too close to the slope of the hill. He hollered for me when he realized he could not back up the incline. Because I was not strong enough to push the heavy tractor back up the hill, he had to hold the brake while I ran for help. Luckily our next-door neighbor was home and came back with me. We both pushed, and Don was able to escape his predicament. As Fred left, he said, "That was a Kodak moment." He could have said a whole lot more. Don was thankful he did not.

Don became more proficient until he eventually mowed the entire lawn. I always worked in my flowers when he mowed, wanting to be available if he ran into trouble. Since Don had only one arm to work with, he could not regulate the speed and turn the steering wheel at the same time. Occasionally he made his turns more quickly than I liked. At times I had to look the other way because I was too scared to watch. However, after Don's first experience on the wet grass, he never had another accident.

Don gained confidence as he drove his John Deere, and he began dreaming of bigger things. Roughly three years after his stroke, Don approached his reading tutor about his desire to drive and asked her to help him. Neither Kay nor I felt comfortable with this idea, but Kay eventually helped Don study the Minnesota driving manual and practice true or false questions.

I did not know if I should encourage Don. I remember praying, "God, please don't let Don pass the test if he will endanger himself or others."

The day came in December 1994, when Don decided he was ready to take his written exam for a driver's permit. He had little experience with computers since his stroke and also had difficulty reading the questions. But Don could listen to the questions read aloud on one of the testing machines and select multiple choice answers. The first time the machine confused Don, and it quit before he finished the test, which meant he flunked.

Don said he learned from his first testing experience, so the following day he took the test again. Although he improved his score by half, he still did not pass. The next day he again walked into the licensing office and took the test a third time.

Don told me, "My desire to drive is much stronger than my need to protect my pride."

This time he passed!

In order to help Don turn more safely with only one hand, a local medical equipment store installed a spinner knob on our steering wheel. The knob must be removed for any other drivers.

The store also bolted a clever, but simple, left foot accelerator to the floor of the van. Don was ready for business.

Mayo's Rehab Department referred us to a man in Rochester who taught brain injury survivors how to drive again. On his first lesson, Don drove around the block for Ray, and I was dumbfounded that he even drove on Broadway, a busy street in Rochester!

Don took five hours of behind-the-wheel instruction. Ray said, "I want to gradually give Don new driving experiences and build up his confidence with small successes." Part of Ray's plan was to have me ride in the backseat while Don took his lessons. The first time I sat in the back, I felt terrorized, but I learned to calm down to scared and finally to just nervous.

Don did not drive with finesse at first. He drove along a street and aimed at a parked car instead of the open lane. When he reached the car, he drove around it, but up to the last moment I wondered if he was going to hit it. For months, he only accelerated or braked and seldom coasted; a ride with him felt very jarring. I generally felt stressed when I rode with Don. For instance, even if I calmly asked if he saw some children walking toward an intersection, he replied in an agitated voice, "I can't talk when I'm concentrating."

We attached convex mirrors to our vehicle's rear-view mirrors to help Don see better behind and beside him. Early on when Don changed lanes, he turned his head quickly to look over his shoulder but kept his eyes focused forward and claimed he had looked. He has good peripheral vision and assured me he had adequately looked, but I was not convinced.

In March 1995, four years after his stroke, Don took his

behind-the-wheel driving test. On his vision test, he could not say the letters correctly, so he traced some of them on the desk. When he took his behind-the-wheel test, he passed the first time! He always knew he would succeed, but I had my doubts. Still, he was determined, or shall I say stubborn?

Don was thrilled to have his license back! At first he drove himself to his reading tutor's home and gradually ventured out by himself more and more.

When Don began to drive himself to his support groups at SEMCIL, he saw friends who needed help and had less independence than he did. Sometimes he gave them rides home after their meetings, which seemed reasonable to Don. However, I worried about him when he did not come home on time. I felt nervous about Don giving rides to other people. Some of them also had mobility issues, and I wondered if he could help them or understand their directions, especially at night. But he always arrived home without incident.

There were times when Don wanted to drive by himself to the home of a new SEMCIL consumer. However, he could not read maps or instructions to navigate to new places. But if his boss at SEMCIL took him to a new consumer the first time, Don could later remember how to find the house on his own.

Don says, "I feel bad for the stress I've caused you because of my stroke. But I also think you worry too much." Many TBI survivors feel guilty about the strain their illnesses put on their spouses, even though they say their spouses worry too much.

Don's Safety

I occasionally worry when Don drives in the winter

because of the snow or ice on our Minnesota roads. Don has promised he will not go out if the roads look dangerous, but he and I don't always agree on the definition of "dangerous."

Don has been careful to drive safely and has not had an accident. However, since I am still nervous when I ride with him, we have settled into a routine in which Don drives when he goes somewhere by himself, but I usually drive when we are together. Especially in the winter, I can drop him off at a door, which is safer and easier than if he drives and has to walk in from a parking lot.

I worry only a little when Don drives on streets after a snowfall since they are quickly plowed and salted. I am more concerned that he could fall on ice when he walks from the van into a building. Although the Americans with Disabilities Act prompted wonderful accommodations for disabled people, I am frustrated at how many handicapped parking spots are not cleared of snow and then turn into a sheet of ice. Businesses do not seem to realize how significant an issue this is for people like Don.

One day Don suddenly realized he had stepped onto a big patch of ice. He froze and did not dare move; he needed help! He's forgotten how he solved that predicament, but he still remembers the panic he felt.

Earlier in Don's recovery, I watched to see how he navigated when he walked on his own. At times he had to ask me for help when he ventured over a slippery spot or when gusts of wind scared him. I worried he might have trouble when he went out alone. Although we still have differences of what we think is safe in the winter, he has not fallen outdoors.

Don fell a couple times inside our house and was able to get up because of what he had learned in physical therapy. However, he recently helped the students at the Mayo PT school and practiced getting up off the floor; we all hoped he will never have to use that skill again, inside or out.

Because Don concentrates so much on his effort to walk, I worry that he is not fully aware of his surroundings. One day as he returned to his van in a parking lot, he walked behind a car but did not see that the driver was about to back up. The driver did not notice Don either. He panicked at the sight of a vehicle coming toward him, but he could not move quickly to get out of the way. The driver fortunately saw Don in time to stop.

Once I watched from a distance as Don set off to enter a gas station. He walked straight toward the door but did not anticipate a challenge. A curb ran the entire front length of the station with ramps at either end. He was headed for trouble because he needed to get to the restroom quickly, and there was nothing for him to hold onto to help him up the step by the door. I had to quickly help Don out of that dilemma. Over time he proved himself more trustworthy. Now he goes out by himself, and I try not to worry about the obstacles he may face.

Adaptive Devices

Commercial adaptive devices help Don compensate for some of his challenges. I also enjoy inventing ways to help him accomplish what he cannot on his own.

Don prefers to wear regular shoes, but he cannot tie his shoelaces with one hand. His PT ordered a pair of little plastic button gadgets to put in one of the top eyelets of each of Don's shoes. They come in black or white. After I tie his shoes tightly, he can loop the lace over or off the little button. I later found some hardware which costs a fraction of the little commercial gadgets. On his tennis shoes, we use a *knurled nut* on the outside of the shoe eyelet and half of a *Chicago screw* (binding screw) on the inside. They are brass and last forever.

When Don first came home, I poured shampoo onto his hand whenever he took a shower. With only one hand, where could he pour the shampoo? Don cannot easily handle a free-standing bottle or pump, so I attached a shampoo pump to the wall of our shower with 3M adhesive strips to give him more independence. He no longer needs help to bathe.

I have tried to get up from a chair with only one foot on the floor, and it is hard work. Don's left leg is exceptionally strong, but his right leg helps him very little when he gets up from a chair. When we changed the flooring in our bathroom, we installed a new toilet that is higher than the standard ones. Don says the extra height makes quite a difference for him.

After Don's legs developed edema, his doctor wanted him to elevate his feet above his heart whenever possible. When we shopped for a recliner, we found that some raise the feet more or less than others, and all of them have the lever on the right side. However, we were able to special order a recliner with the lever on the *left* side. That allowed Don to control the footrest independently. He also controls the edema in his legs with heavy-duty elastic stockings that his doctor prescribed.

Don usually grabs the doorframe when he enters a house. To make this easier and safer for Don at home, I attached a sturdy handle with long heavy screws on the outside trim of either side of our doorframe. Don can hold onto a handle when he climbs the two steps in or out of our house. Although I have offered to put up handicap grab bars in our walk-in shower, Don says he manages fine with the bar that is already there.

Our answering machine is a valuable tool, especially when I am gone and Don answers the phone. Since he may get information mixed up, Don frequently asks people to call back and leave a message for me. Don can tell me the gist of a phone conversation, but the answering machine ensures that we get the correct details of a message.

Compensation

When Don finds he cannot accomplish something, he tries to make it happen a different way. He has learned many compensation skills. When he goes down a stairway without a railing on the left side, he turns around, grabs the rail on the right, and backs down. Don sometimes starts a story and asks me to finish it to ensure that the facts are accurate. It appears that some of Don's deficits are not going to improve, so compensation is the only option.

When I think of the severity of Don's stroke and look at the MRI of his brain (see photo), I am amazed that he has successfully conquered many challenges in his life. He is remarkable, and I am very proud of him.

What has helped us cope and given us hope:

- Medications have controlled Don's seizures and other symptoms.

- Don used a pool noodle with straps for swimming.
- A pedal with strapped platform has allowed Don to ride a stationary recumbent exercise bike.
- We added cable TV to our exercise room.
- A test for driving readiness was available through the occupational therapy department.
- We adapted our vehicles for Don with a spinner knob, left foot accelerator, and convex rear-view mirrors.
- Specialized driving instruction was available for brain injury survivors.
- A handicapped parking sticker and well-maintained, accessible accommodations at businesses make a big difference.
- Shoe buttons have made dressing easier for Don.
- A wall mounted shampoo dispenser has allowed Don to bathe independently.
- We installed a higher toilet in our bathroom to help Don get up easier.
- Don special ordered a left-handled recliner.
- Grab bars have provided safety.
- Don learned to back down staircases that have no left railing.
- An answering machine or voicemail has allowed us to receive accurate recorded phone messages.
- Don has learned to defer to me at times for details.

Chapter 10
Rosella's Inner Struggles

Although I have already included many of my memories and feelings, I want to share some of my inner struggles that I am rather embarrassed to tell. Don and I at times have seen our issues and challenges from differing perspectives. Those difficult times are not easy to expose to others. We normally consider ourselves an open book; we want to be transparent. However, not all is pretty.

Don is such a dear and wonderful person. He has dealt with a tragedy in life in a stellar way. He was a man of character when I married him and he still is. I love him and he loves me. We often tell each other how glad we are to be married to each other. But Don and I struggle every day because of his stroke.

When to Help

People with disabilities usually want to do as much as possible for themselves. However, I cannot always anticipate when Don wants assistance and when he does not. When this issue frustrated me a while back, I decided to mentally tally how often I could be wrong. I became convinced that if I asked Don if he wanted help, he would say, "No," and if I did not ask him, he would say in a somewhat aggravated manner, "HELP me!" He has lost control of so much in his life that I wonder if his reaction is a subconscious attempt to regain some power of choice.

Don struggles to pull the two sides of his pants together and button them with only his left hand. For years I never knew when I should automatically help him, when I should ask if he wanted help, or when he did not want me say or do anything. On many occasions, I guessed incorrectly. Some time ago, we finally settled into a routine in which Don usually asks me to help him button his pants if I am near. When he is alone, he leans against the dresser to support one side of his pants while he buttons them, or he lies down on his back on the bed to accomplish the task.

Don has learned to completely dress himself. He buttons his long-sleeved shirts on the loosest button and then bites the cuff as he undresses. He can even put on his *industrial strength* elastic stockings with one hand; I have a hard time pulling his stockings up when I use two hands.

Another challenge is how to assist Don when he walks. I was taught to steady him by grabbing onto his belt if he felt insecure. Crowds, wind, or long distances can make him apprehensive. Between his fear and my desire to support him, we slipped into a pattern early on in which he grabbed my right arm for security. Over the years my back and shoulder suffered because of this. But we just could not help ourselves; he simply needed support.

Recently we discovered another way to assist him and still save my body. Don grabs *my* belt or waistband when he needs assistance. In a certain position, his knuckles give me a back spasm, but if he holds on toward my side, the technique works well for both of us. PTs do not like this and prefer I grab his belt instead. However, I most frequently revert to offer him my arm.

Beyond the communications and physical limitations Don and I deal with, I have issues that are uniquely mine.

Personal Health

Caregiving takes a toll. I care for Don because I love him, but our daily stress affects my body and my emotions. In the early years, I did not always have the energy or insight to balance caring for Don and our children as well as myself; I let my needs fall to the bottom of my priorities. I did not exercise as I should, and I sometimes hurt myself when I did the heavy jobs Don used to do. People say I look younger than I am, but that is not always how I feel. Over the years, I have often agreed when Don says, "We're a wreck."

After I hit forty, in addition to taking Don to Mayo, I frequently went there for my own healthcare. I had surgeries for a thyroid nodule, two cataracts, a colon polyp, and a neuroma on my foot. I had to tolerate some of these medical conditions for a year or two before they became significant enough to treat. I dealt with back and shoulder pain because I helped Don less carefully than I should have or continued activities inappropriate for my age.

Once I missed the bottom step to our basement and broke my foot. We were quite a sight when we walked around in our shorts, Don with a brace and a cane, and I with a cast and crutches. Several years ago, I talked with my doctor about feeling overwhelmed all the time and not sleeping well. The antidepressant he prescribed improved my outlook and enabled me to focus and to sleep better. My cholesterol is up; my bone density is down. Shoot, I really am a wreck!

Concern about Don's Health

I hate to admit that I worry. However, underlying anxiety about Don's health weighs on me. When he first came home from the hospital, I used to wonder if he could have another stroke. Many times when I drove into the garage, I stopped for a moment to gather myself before I went into the house, wondering if I might find Don dead or alive. That passed after a year or two; however, I still worry about his health.

I worry when I hear a leak from his *CPAP*, the machine that treats his sleep apnea by providing *continuous positive air pressure* through a face mask when he sleeps. A few years ago, Don apparently was not receiving an adequate supply of oxygen when he slept, even though he already used a CPAP. His body responded by producing more red blood cells to carry oxygen. However, this caused his blood to become so thick he could have eventually had another stroke. To treat this, Don's doctors increased his CPAP pressure and ordered *phlebotomies*, blood draws that removed enough red blood cells to thin his blood.

Don's weight concerns me. I watch him order fried JoJo potatoes and worry about his vascular system or his gallbladder. His weight gain has caused him to need medication for hypertension, and his doctor says Don is prediabetic. When I have to buy him a larger size of clothes, I wonder if I will be able to lift him if he becomes bedridden and needs more care.

Some people show their love through food. People feel compelled to give food to Don. They give him heaping piles at a potluck and push extra cookies or desserts on him. They are trying to be nice. However, the more he eats, the more he gains, and the less active he becomes.

I suspect that part of the reason Don has occasional fungal infections is that when he showers he tends not to wipe the left side of his body dry and begins the day with damp clothes. Years before his stroke, Don acquired a toenail fungus. Several years after his stroke, he developed a raging fungal infection on his leg under his AFO, his plastic ankle brace. His dermatologist put Don on a strong antifungal medication for many months until his leg healed and his toenail grew out.

Some time ago, doctors diagnosed Don with an *abdominal aortic aneurysm*. That is a weakened bulge in the main artery that comes down from his heart. Don gets regular scans and may eventually need a stent. My mother's aortic aneurysm ruptured when she was seventy-nine; and at the time, her friends thought she was given a wonderful way to die. But I am not eager for Don to leave me prematurely!

When Don struggles with intense back pain, I feel bad for him. His back used to "go out" occasionally, but each time he recovered in a few days. During an episode of back spasms a couple years ago, his pain was so intense he could not even sit on the edge of the bed for four days and could not leave the house for a week. I had to completely change my schedule. More importantly, those episodes of back pain are difficult and discouraging for Don.

Physical therapists gave Don some exercises to strengthen his back, and he switched to riding a recumbent bike instead of walking. We are both relieved his back has improved, but we wonder what the future holds.

A few years ago Don experienced amnesia. The first time, he sat down for breakfast and started speaking in a confused manner. I soon realized he did not remember the previous day or anything from the recent past. This lasted about half an hour, after which he could remember everything. That first episode scared me because I thought he might be having another stroke. However, when his tests in the ER did not show any new stroke activity, they dismissed him for later follow-up testing.

Don had a few of these amnesia events; they all happened at the same time of the day and lasted half an hour. Each time I thought, *Here we go again.* I asked him a few questions about the previous day, but he had no recall. I learned to reassure Don that these spells had happened before and always passed. Don did not lose consciousness, but the episodes were unsettling for both of us. After the Mayo doctors tested him extensively, they ruled out any major neurological or cardiac causes and diagnosed his episodes as *transient global amnesia.*

All these conditions have been medical realities and legitimate reasons for my anxiety about Don's health. I ache for Don when he does not feel well, but I need to control my worry.

Another chronic concern I have is that Don could easily fall. Although Don was nervous at first about walking in crowds, he gained confidence and skill over time. He has not taken any falls on ice as I feared, but he fell a few times in our house.

Once when he sat down on the toilet, he did not realize he was off center because he could not feel anything on his right side. Down he went on the floor. He did the same thing on a chair one time. These were scary experiences for both of us—not at all comical.

One day Don decided to slip forward off his chair and lie on the living room floor to rest. He had never done this before, and on the way down he lost his balance and tipped over. He broke two fingers on his paralyzed hand in that fall.

I am not the only one who worries about Don falling. Often people warn him to be careful as he enters their homes. Don replies, "Don't worry! I'll just fall and sue." Some people laugh, and others do not appreciate his humor.

Occasionally we encounter tension between Don's desire for independence and my concern about his safety. There are times he wants to attempt new activities he has not yet demonstrated his ability to perform. If I ask him to try parts of the whole, to show me his abilities, he replies, "I sometimes want to decide things myself. I think I can do it."

I worry that Don thinks his desire to undertake a task constitutes his ability to accomplish it. If he hurts himself and loses more mobility, I will have a hard time caring for him and lifting him, or he might end up in a nursing home. If he has an accident and hurts others, we will both feel awful.

I know I am not the only spouse of a brain injury survivor who worries. Although I do not worry all the time, I have to admit to times when fear and concern come over me. Those episodes usually come in waves and focus on a specific activity or issue for Don.

When I worry, I sometimes envision the worst scenario, from an accident, through suffering, to a nursing home, and finally to death. I realize those things happen, and my worrying does not help anything. However, this little process purges my worry and helps me "let go" and "let" Don try things. But I have varied degrees of success. Our reality is that our lives are not normal; on occasion I have reason to worry and draw limits.

House Maintenance

I have always loved to figure out how things work. Instead of paying a maintenance person, I like to fix things myself. I learned many life skills from my dad and from a girls' shop course in high school. Don would much rather fix things around the house himself than watch me struggle with them, but that is not the way things work anymore.

I have learned how to keep track of the service for our cars, change oil on our lawn tractor and snow blower, change parts in toilet tanks and faucets, maintain the furnace, and fix appliances. Screws on things say to me, "Take me apart." Because I like to fix things, Don surprised me with my own DeWalt cordless drill for Christmas one year. I enjoyed his choice, so I guess I am not a typical wife.

There are times when Don helps me fix things. When the spring on the dishwasher door broke, he helped me stretch the new one into place. Other times he holds something for me or gives advice. He is always my cheerleader. Even though I feel satisfaction when I accomplish some of these tasks, I would willingly give them up if Don could do them. Household maintenance mingles stress and satisfaction for me.

To-Do Lists

Every stay-at-home mom has been tempted, after an exhausting day with the kids, to launch into a to-do list for her husband the minute he arrives home from work. I learned years ago that our marriage would benefit if I disciplined myself to delay my requests for at least a little while. Since Don's stroke, our tables have turned. When I enter a room, Don sometimes starts reciting a list of tasks he wants me to do. He is unable to do many things himself, so in my absence he creates his mental list for me. Before I finish his first request, he wants me to start the second, but he also gets frustrated when I do not finish tasks. I need to stop, listen, write down the list, and have him help me prioritize.

I cannot always distinguish if what Don says is an opinion or a demand. Before we make a decision, I like to discuss the pros and cons. But Don expresses his opinions in such a strong way that I feel domineering if I raise another side of the issue. Our psychologist told me I need to learn to be more assertive. He suggested I read the book *Your Perfect Right*, by Albert Emmons. I wonder if I will ever learn how to better express kind assertiveness without feeling that I am sparring or demanding my way.

Don often anticipates what I am about to do by half a step. When he rode with me, he used to reach for the garage door opener just before I did or tell me to turn off the headlights just as I touched the switch. He beat me to the tasks before I could accomplish them, and I felt his actions or comments implied I was incompetent. Don has gotten better about not doing that. As I am about to put bread in the toaster at breakfast, he is one step ahead of me and asks me to do it. Or I walk into the kitchen before lunch or dinner, and Don suggests what I should cook. There are times I long to gaze into the freezer and decide for myself what to cook, like I did when he was working. I hate to admit that I let these little things irritate me at times.

Poor Judgment

I agonize at times when Don is completely oblivious to his impaired judgment. When our grandkids were little, he offered to watch them, but he could not have kept up to their speed or physically kept them out of trouble. He has insisted on going out alone for an appointment in six inches of new snow. He has begged me to let him mow the grass or blow the snow when he cannot even walk on grass or ice without help, let alone work two sets of hand controls.

Once after his stroke, Don wanted to invest in the grain futures. Since he regularly says things differently than he means and cannot read or do math well, and since I do not know anything in this arena and have no interest in learning, I felt it was an incredibly bad idea. That time I asserted my wishes.

Don went through a phase in which he wanted to swim without his floatation device. I am sure his paralyzed side would have sunk, and I was not strong enough to bring him up from the bottom of the pool. There were also times when he wanted me to arrange for him to do public speaking at SEMCIL, at our camp, or at a mission office where he used to consult. However, his thought patterns were not organized, and even if I wrote notes for him, he could not read them.

One day Don drove up to the McDonald's drive-through

window to buy an ice cream cone. He did not anticipate how he could both steer the car and hold an ice cream cone with only one hand. When judgment issues like these occur, a crushing feeling grips my chest.

My Personal Needs and Self-Image

People do not realize how their offhand comments may be insensitive or uninformed. Once someone scolded me, "You have to let him try things." I felt judged because that person had little understanding of our situation or of Don's limitations. Another time, someone rode with him shortly after he had obtained his driver's license. Before they left, I told the person to watch and let Don know of any danger he might not appear to recognize. I felt chided when the person responded, "Oh, I would never tell him how to drive!" I should ignore such comments, but I struggle not to take them personally.

There is such a fine line between wise caution and overprotection. I often wonder if I am dealing with Don in the best way possible. Although I do not want to be a controlling person, I vacillate on where I should draw that line. I know I slip off balance and need advice at times, but I prefer a discussion directly with Don or people close to us instead of unsolicited advice from people on the periphery.

Because I want to allow Don to make choices, I give in to what he wants from time to time against my better judgment. On occasion I cope with the stress of doing that by detaching myself emotionally. But if I pull away frequently, I feel the bottom of my emotional cup is cut off and my emotions are all drained out; obviously that is not a good coping mechanism.

However, I heard that a doctor friend of ours says, "Don't mess with people's coping mechanisms." I guess we have to do the best we can with whatever works.

Emotional Health

You may not think we are emotionally healthy at this point. But in spite of all we have disclosed about ourselves, I think both Don and I are reasonably healthy. We have dealt with a lot of stress and have not crumbled.

There are times I am more emotionally flat than either sad or depressed. That feeling can wear me out and overwhelm me. It hampers my ability to start a project or concentrate. I also wear out when I give and initiate excessively.

Don and I have talked about how we are wired differently and periodically need a break from each other. A day home alone refreshes me, and I am grateful Don understands this. He goes stir-crazy if he does not leave the house regularly, so he tries to schedule at least one reason to get out every day. He has several lunch dates each week. For many years, I have gone out for lunch once a week with some friends. It is cheaper than getting therapy and more fun.

While Don loves to talk with other people, there are times he has a hard time carrying on conversation with me. That makes me feel distant. We can drive for miles, and I am the only one who initiates conversation. I long for him to ask me about my thoughts like he did so well before his stroke. We all feel good when someone asks us to express our ideas. Those encounters make me feel close to someone, especially my husband. Or I wish Don would do what I want now and then, just to make me happy. Our relationship has changed.

There are also things that I wish he would not do that help me feel closer to him. I wish Don would not fuss about remembering names, instead acknowledge his problem and go on. I wish he would not dig himself a hole by claiming to understand everything when he does not realize how much information he gets mixed up. I am sure there are also many things Don wishes I would or would not do!

What to Expose

As Don talked about writing a book, one obstacle in my mind was the question of how much to reveal about the painful parts in our lives. On one hand, I hesitated to divulge some of the issues I have written about here. On the other hand, I did not want to pretend everything has been easy or make stroke or TBI survivors think they are the only ones who struggle with similar issues.

I suspect our transparency may be helpful for someone who has a similar situation in life; we are willing to share for that reason. However, I feel slightly concerned about exposing some of our private, or weaker, or even embarrassing sides to people we know.

In traumatic brain injury workshops, we have learned that all TBI survivors have their own unique deviation from normal behavior or function. Each individual, couple, or family has their own distinct struggles. I am grateful that, for the most part, Don's personality is much the same as before his stroke. He is a wonderfully pleasant, kind, and generous person.

I have little to complain about in comparison with many

"normal" spouses. We love each other and have committed to work at our marriage and life's obstacles. But marriage takes more determination and grace in our post-stroke phase of life. When the book is printed, we will see where the line falls on what we choose to expose. As you read this, we hope you will have the kindness to glean what is meaningful to you and blow the chaff away.

What helps me cope and gives me hope:

- Don is such a dear person and I am proud of him. I love him and he loves me.
- Between the two of us, we figure out how we can accomplish what he cannot on his own.
- I try to be careful to protect my body when I help Don.
- I try not to worry about Don, but I realize I am not the only one with concerns.
- When I need to take on tasks Don used to do, I try to think of them as challenges and enjoy the satisfaction I get when I accomplish them.
- When Don has a list of things he wants me to do, I try to have him prioritize them.
- I sometimes have to let go and allow Don to try things even when I am worried about his judgment.
- We regularly take a break from each other.
- We have both committed to work at our marriage and life's obstacles.

Chapter 11

More About Our Family

Since I introduced you to our family, I want to tell you a bit more about each of us.

Jon Died from Cancer

Jon told his wife that since he was so near the end of high school when Don had his stroke, he probably focused more on moving on to college than on our family situation. He told her about his frustration when roles flipped, and he felt he had to act like a father to both Josh and his dad. But for the most part, Jon said life went on quite normally, and he did not dwell on Don's stroke. Jon always treated Don with love and respect. We were proud of his maturity, how he handled the changes that came into his life because of Don's illness.

After Jon graduated from college in Chicago, he went directly on to medical school. A year before finishing medical school he married Svea, a wonderful gal he had known as he grew up. Jon was finishing his family practice residency when he was diagnosed with stage IV chondrosarcoma in 2003. He and Svea had a delightful little two-year-old son, Ben, and Svea was pregnant after having a miscarriage that spring. Jon and Svea were excited about moving back to Rochester where he looked forward to working as a family practice physician. They were having a home built when he found out he was sick.

Once in the early days of his illness, Jon said to Svea, "If I die next week, do you want to remember this as a sad, horrible week or as a wonderful week?" That set the tone for how they lived the rest of his life. Jon was able to enjoy the second half of each of his months of chemo; move into their new home and settle his family; participate in the birth of their second son, Drew; build a fort in the basement for his kids; and spend a lot of time with Svea and the boys. Although his illness and death caused all of us wrenching pain, Jon made many wonderful memories for us. He made a valiant effort to make the best of his last months.

Jon had to endure thoracic surgery to diagnose his specific cancer and then undergo six months of chemo. Later he had a craniotomy to treat metastases to his brain. However, throughout his illness, he never complained. His character, his faith in God, his wonderful wife, his two darling little boys, and a host of supporters helped him through eight difficult, but good months. He died tragically early at the age of twenty-nine, just shy of beginning a career he had worked hard to reach. We remember him with great joy and sadness and are tremendously proud of him.

Two years after Jon's death, Svea met a wonderful man who also had lost his spouse to cancer. They were married and have blended into a large and busy new family. This development in Svea's and our grandsons' lives brings us joy. We miss Jon, but we are thrilled that Svea again has a spouse, and our grandsons have a daddy as well as new siblings. They live nearby and have chosen to keep us in their lives. When we lost Jon, we also could have lost his family, but we still have them—and more.

Josh's Adventures

Don's stroke caused Josh to suddenly mature. Stroke survival dynamics were part of his life for six years before he left for college. Josh was always a confident kid, and he survived the difficult changes in his life with grace. I am sure there were situations when he and Jon felt embarrassed about their dad's limitations; however, they never outwardly showed their embarrassment, even though they certainly could have.

Josh says, "I didn't want to shame my dad or hurt my mom by making a big deal out of our situation. I couldn't explain things so my friends would understand, so I hurt for a while and later let things go. The pain usually didn't last much past the moment because I loved my dad. We were often caught in tension between our love for Dad and our frustrations."

In his high school years, Josh learned to play guitar, sang in two choirs, worked at our Bible camp, enjoyed church youth activities, and loved to initiate group activities with his friends. At his high school graduation, he gave a speech in which he told the audience that, in addition to all he had learned in school, he had also learned from his dad never to give up. Josh recalls:

I don't think we felt bitterness about our circumstances. Dad had taught us to accept things we couldn't change and go on with life. But that wasn't always easy. One Christmas after Dad's stroke, the tree needed to be decorated. Mom was busy, and I didn't really want to trim the tree. We decided, "This stinks," and we all ended up crying. That memory hurts to this day, and trimming the Christmas tree is still a struggle for me.

I look back and see good things that have come out of our difficult times. I know from personal life experience that the value of a person goes way beyond their accomplishments or limitations. What matters most is who they are inside, how they treat other people, and the relationships they establish with others. In that respect, Dad ranks way up there. I have a great dad and mom. People look up to them. They maintain their dignity even in the midst of difficult circumstances. I am proud of them.

Josh studied philosophy and political science in college. During his junior year, he spent a semester in the Middle East. He met Beth Hudson at college and they were married the summer after he graduated. She is also a delightful daughter-in-law; both our boys chose wonderful wives.

After Josh and Beth were married, they moved to the East Coast, where Josh worked in politics and Beth worked for an international aid organization. Two years later, they moved to the Middle East to study Arabic for a year. When they returned to the States, Josh worked as a researcher at an international affairs think tank while Beth earned a master's degree. Beth is a graphic designer, and Josh works for an organization that assists developing democracies.

Don did not have enough stamina for a trip when Josh and Beth's little son was born; but while I traveled for a week of grandma time, Don stayed home and survived all on his own.

While their baby was still little, they flew here on a surprise visit to introduce their son to Don. Between trips, we enjoy each other on video Skype.

We took our boys on some of our overseas trips, and Beth is a child of missionaries, so both sets of parents cultivated the seeds of international interest in our children. We feel pretty certain they will not end up near home. And actually, although we worry a little, we join in their excitement as they venture into the future. We want them to be where they feel they should be, and we will support them.

Rosella—Helping Don and Other People

Although we are all glad I was able to stay home as our boys grew up, I sometimes wondered what I might do if I ever needed to work; I had decided I did not want to go back to nursing. In 2002 when our church offered me a part-time job, we quickly realized that it was a good fit for me. Among other responsibilities, I met with new people and helped integrate them into our congregation. Many of my tasks involved caring for and encouraging people, which was fulfilling for me.

I felt overwhelmed the spring after Jon died. When Jon was sick, I had gotten behind in life; and when I was both grieving and working, I could not catch up. So I took a leave of absence to rest; spend more time with Don, Svea, Ben, and Drew; catch up on communication with friends; and work on this book. Three-months later, I returned to work feeling more emotionally healthy. However, I later retired after working for the church for six years.

Despite our tragedies, I often ponder how good our

life really is. Don had his stroke and our son Jon died; yet all along, we have been surrounded with love and support. We live in safety, have plenty to eat, and have a lovely home. We often get to spend time with Svea and Steve and our delightful grandchildren. The greatest gift we can give Jon is to care for his family, and we find great joy in doing this. While Josh and Beth have lived far away from us, we talk with them frequently and travel to visit each other. Our lives are not all bad.

Because of our life experiences, we seem to have license to jump quickly into the lives of people who are struggling. Our suffering has given us freedom and boldness to relate to people we may not have felt free to approach earlier in our lives. Life is difficult—but good. We have lost much, but we still have each other, and we treasure relationships with many wonderful people.

Don Plods Along

Don is a plodder, not a sprinter or a person with flash. When he faces a challenge, he trudges through it slowly, slogging along until he finishes. That is the way he handled graduate school and many other situations in his life, including his stroke. He just kept plodding along, determined to improve. There is a fine line between stubbornness and determination.

Recovery is a process rather than an event in time. Over the twenty years since his stroke, Don has seen much improvement. In recent years, he has plateaued in his recovery; he no longer sees much progress. However, he recently noticed a small change. When he rides his recumbent bike, he can finally keep his right leg from flopping outward, without grabbing his pants leg. That means his leg is stronger than even six months ago. These days, Don generally looks for ways to compensate more than for ways to improve. He keeps plodding along.

Health concerns sporadically surface for Don. Not long ago, he added a pill for hypertension to his medication routine. We were encouraged that the last tests for his abdominal aortic aneurysm showed no change in size, but they will continue to check him. Since Don does not have as much energy as he did a few years ago, he has to take more naps, and he realizes he is slowing down. He becomes winded more frequently and grunts and groans when he exerts himself.

Don's most recent health challenge came as recurrent spells of three to four days when he was so nauseous, dizzy, and exhausted that he had to sleep for most of the time. After extensive testing turned up nothing, his doctor told Don gradually to eliminate the pill he took to stop him from kicking in his sleep. That solved the problem. The drug's side effects had robbed Don of his quality of life for several months. He feels much better, and we can again make plans for activities with more confidence.

Don likes to keep busy. He still loves going out for meals or visiting with friends. He also enjoys a men's small group as well as our couples' care group. Every day, he tries to plan some reason to interact with people. Many times in the last few years, he has listened to the entire Bible on CD and followed along in his Bible. Since he has the time, he prays daily for a long list of friends and relatives.

Don loves to spend time with our immediate family, and being a grandpa brings him special joy. He wishes he could read books to our grandkids, but he cannot. However, before the youngest ones learned to read, he discovered that they enjoyed the *I Spy* books, in which he could name objects in a collage and have the kids to find them. Even though his interaction with his grandkids is not what he wishes it could be, he enjoys watching me play with them or take care of them. We have flown to visit Josh and Beth, but those trips have become increasingly complicated and exhausting for Don.

Don's stroke and Jon's death were difficult and painful times. However, in both cases we had many resources to draw on: quality life lessons and experiences; support of family and friends; a stable marriage with loving children; financial security; and faith in a loving God. We had a wealth of tools to use in our crises.

Because of Don's stroke, we have each struggled through many challenges. While life is not easy, we have had many good times in the midst of our difficulties. We continue to trudge along and have concluded that *there IS life after stroke.*

What helps us cope and gives us hope:

When we tend to feel sad about our losses, we think instead of our two wonderful sons and their families, the love Don and I have for each other, our many good memories, the activities that still give us fulfillment, the wonderful people we call friends, and of what God means in our lives.

Chapter 12
Lessons We Have Learned

Many of our early life lessons helped us deal with Don's stroke. We also learned much from his stroke experience. At times, matters were in order and played out well. Other times we learned the hard way.

Don's dad, Ray, farmed and taught his four children how to work hard. Among the many other lessons his parents taught, Don's mom, Ruth, instilled in her children the desire for education. For six summers after he turned thirteen years old, Don moved to the farm of Orien and Elaine Klath and worked for them. Don learned from Orien's example to react in a calm and strong way to difficulties and not to waste energy on anger. Don incorporated into his life many qualities he admired in Orien and Elaine. When Don faced recovery, he already knew how to work hard, and he wanted to learn how to get better rather than dwell on anger.

The classes Don took at North Dakota State University in Fargo prepared him academically for life, but he probably learned as much from his extracurricular activities. In the NDSU Concert Choir, he learned the discipline and the joy of striving for excellence. At FarmHouse Fraternity, he made good friends who have stuck by us for almost four decades. Through InterVarsity Christian Fellowship, he grew in his faith and in leadership skills. As Don worked at his recovery, he understood that practice brings rewarding results. He also knew he had well-established relationships with friends and with God, so he could lean on them when he needed support.

Don and I met through InterVarsity Christian Fellowship. We enjoyed many of the same interests and shared common values. After we married, Don worked as a youth director and I as a registered nurse in northwestern Wisconsin. I quit nursing after our first son, Jonathan, was born, but my medical knowledge and experience later helped me understand the terms Don's doctors used and helped me care for Don.

Shortly after Jon was born, we moved to Pakistan where we worked as houseparents at a boarding school for missionary children. During that year and nine months, we experienced a new culture and worked with people from around the world. We once watched two men use a single shovel, one lifting with the handle and the other helping to lift the load with a rope tied down near the blade. Through that experience and many others, we discovered that our way of doing things was not the only way. When a standard method did not work for Don during his rehab, we tried to think of other ways to solve the problem.

When we came back to the States, Don wanted to become a psychologist. He earned his master's degree in Counseling and Guidance from the University of North Dakota in Grand Forks. Our son Josh was born the year Don interned at a counseling center in Seattle, Washington. Don returned to UND to finish his PhD.

During his years of graduate school, Don learned skills to help people who were hurting. When he finished school, we moved to Rochester, Minnesota, where he started a private counseling practice. Within months, he developed a full caseload of clients. He loved his work and later applied many of his problem-solving skills to his own life.

We learned early in our marriage that our happiness depended much more on our relationships and our faith than on how much money we had. Our boys brought us great pride and joy. They gave us reason to keep going after Don's stroke. Our families and friends, as well as our Christian faith, supported us when Don's stroke knocked us down. Our frugality during Don's grad school years had not hurt us at the time and paid off after Don was disabled.

We did not always make perfect decisions, but many life lessons and many of our earlier choices helped us deal with the tragedy of Don's stroke. For example, our transitions were much easier because our lives were relatively simplified and not stretched to the limit.

Throughout our marriage, we made it a priority to contribute to our church, missions, and other charities. Having lived in another culture, we knew the stresses missionaries encounter. After Don started his practice, we decided to save enough money so that he could take a trip overseas each year to lecture and offer counseling for missionaries. Our kids and I went with him on some of his trips.

Don says, "I enjoyed counseling missionaries. Like many people, they had difficulties, but their stressful living situations exacerbated them. I used to go and counsel for a week or two and then get out of there before I became part of the problem."

We rarely differed in how we spent money. Every time

Don went overseas alone, he filled out a loan application from our bank and left it with me. It summarized our current financial records in case something happened to him. What a gift! When I suddenly had to take over the finances, everything was in order, and I could figure out how to manage.

Don found great satisfaction providing for our family, and he wanted the boys and me well supported if he could not care for us. For that reason, we spent money each month on disability insurance. That discipline hurt minimally at the time but saved us financially when we needed help.

When Don started his psychology practice, we chose not to significantly change our lifestyle. We had lived on relatively little early in our marriage. After Don started counseling, we soon had much more discretionary income. However, we deliberately chose to live below our means, to live more simply than our income permitted.

The house we lived in while Don finished grad school was adequate for us. A year after we arrived in Rochester, we built a house that was only slightly larger than our previous house. We are thankful that, on top of the traumatic changes that suddenly hit us, we did not have to default on a large mortgage and lose our house.

Don easily accessed our walkout rambler, at first by using a ramp and later by climbing the two steps in from the garage. He met all his basic needs on our main floor and did not have to go downstairs regularly to the boys' bedrooms and our family room. While Don was in the hospital, other patients talked about their need to sell or remodel their homes because they were no longer accessible for them. Our choice to build a modest, adaptable, and handicapped-accessible home paid us many benefits after Don's stroke.

Don even kept his business simple. When Ken Wadum joined Don's practice, they shared expenses and did not create a complicated business structure. That arrangement helped Ken and the secretaries when they wrapped up Don's practice.

When my dad was hospitalized and dying, my mom said, "No individual friend could have carried us through this experience. God prompted one person one day and someone else another day to come alongside and encourage us." When Don and I needed a support system, our family, our current friends, and friends from our past rallied to care for us. Although no one was there all the time, they all fit together to love and support us.

People were creative in helping us. While Don was in the hospital, a small group of ladies we knew well had a coffee party at our house and cleaned it once a week. Folks gave us food, and I especially appreciated when I did not have to keep track of and return containers. Friends also gave our family gift certificates to restaurants near the hospital. A number of friends invited our boys to do things with their families; that was a wonderful gift as well.

We soon recognized our need to accept help from others, not only for our good, but for theirs. Our friends talked about how they hurt, watching us struggle, and they wanted to do something for us. We realized we could not possibly thank people adequately or pay them back for their kindness. We could only thank them on the spot and hope to later pass the kindness on to someone else.

Not everyone has a lot of friends or a loving family to come to their aid when tragedy strikes. However, since Don's stroke, we have made new friends through support groups, church activities, and volunteering. We benefit when we become active in organizations where quality people are involved. In the end, when we try to befriend someone, we soon gain a friend.

Although I appreciated people's concern when Don first had his stroke, I became exhausted from constantly retelling our story. So I borrowed an answering machine and recorded a message that said, "I'm really tired and, if I'm home, I may not have energy to answer the phone. Please leave a message and then call... I will keep these three people informed." That really helped me. Now patients have many more communication options available to keep friends and family informed in a crisis.

Don and I have always wanted to be transparent with others. We find that sharing ourselves is helpful both to us and to our friends. Although that works for us, not everyone is wired for transparency, and some have legitimate reasons to protect their privacy. Right after Don's stroke, I was reeling from my increasing awareness of all Don could not do. I needed people outside our inner circle of family and friends to allow us privacy and be sensitive to Don's condition and my emotions.

Many people wonder what to do or say in traumatic situations. That fear can scare them off from even coming to visit. Most of our family and friends helped in comforting ways. We found that the most helpful thing people did was simply to tell us they cared, whether by a visit, a hug, a card, or a phone call.

Visitors sometimes voiced their own assumptions and said, "We know you're tired so we won't stay long." I preferred if they asked, "How are you feeling today? How long do you want us to stay? Let us know if you become tired." If Don had stamina, he loved to have friends stay. If he was tired, a long conversation exhausted him. Our most helpful visitors *asked* us what we wanted, *listened* to what we said, *believed* us, and *followed* our direction.

While Don tended to take whatever came along, I had more difficulty dealing with some *less than helpful* visits. I felt especially drained when I listened to people struggle with why this all had happened to Don. I had concluded there was no answer to that question. While I recognized their struggle, I felt drained to listen to other people process that question for themselves or try to explain their answer to us. People say the darndest things.

A few times, people were determined to help us in the way *they* felt was useful, rather than ask or sense if what they offered really was helpful to us. Even if people really wanted to help, I did not always have the emotional strength to figure out what they could do for us or to allow casual acquaintances to do personal tasks for us. What I may have normally considered important was not a priority for me during our crisis.

I once heard someone chide my friend who was in crisis, saying, "You need to learn to accept help from people." Someone who makes such a declaration may not know the whole picture, and despite its good intent, that statement judges a vulnerable person. It also can focus more on the needs of the person offering their help than on the person in need.

Another time, I heard a man say that he had helped some people financially, but he did not like the way they used his gift or choices they made. I felt vulnerable and wondered if people were judging us. I was living emotionally on the edge, and at that time little things bothered me more than normal.

Even though Don and I both enjoy visiting and laughing, we do not enjoy conversations that are hyped up a lot. When Don was sick, we appreciated visits that were lower key. We enjoyed dialogues more than monologues, and meaningful conversations more than excessive sympathy or hype.

Especially in the first days after Don's stroke, I felt a need to be with him. I went home in the evenings to be with the boys, but I did not want to be away from Don for long during the day. Even though I knew he was being well cared for, I had an emotional need to be near him. A number of times when people invited me out for lunch, I wanted to return quickly to Don's room. Until he was more stable, I did not feel comfortable chatting for long periods of time away from him.

There was not much opportunity for us to be close to each other in the hospital. We missed touching each other. One day I crawled up beside Don on his bed so we could soak up a little comfort from each other. In walked a visitor. Since that experience, I have offered to guard the hospital door for friends who need some close time together. Although doctors and hospital staff cannot stand around waiting for their patients, private moments are important for a patient and spouse's emotional well-being.

Both Don and I want to be close to each other. I especially crave gentle touch, a hug, or his hand on my shoulder. But since Don struggles with balance and needs his cane, he cannot easily offer touch or a hug. Instead, he leans somewhat forward and waits for me to hug him. I would love to sit close to Don on our couch. However, he always sits in his recliner because he can lay back to elevate his feet and more easily get up from it.

Our favorite time to soak up togetherness is before we get up in the morning. We can just hold each other, and Don does not have to fight for balance. I also savor the times when I sit on his left side at church and he puts his arm on my shoulder.

When our communication breaks down, we feel disconnected from each other. If one of us calls the shots too much, or I point out Don's shortcomings, our closeness easily eludes us. A harsh response can make us feel suddenly distant. We continually have to work to foster gentleness and emotional closeness between us.

After his stroke, Don experienced changes in his sexual function. Changes in intimacy after a brain injury can become a huge adjustment for both spouses. Some challenges are physical and others are mental or a matter of communication. Even though a conversation can be difficult, people who have had stroke or TBI might benefit from a discussion about sexual difficulties with a physician or psychologist. Along with other TBI survivors, we concluded that good advice on sexuality with disability is hard to find; I still have not read anything I thought was particularly helpful.

Humor has helped us through many tough times. Don

frequently jokes and we laugh together; he has always loved to tease. After Don came home from the hospital, we developed the habit of watching *M*A*S*H* while I fixed supper. We enjoyed that daily dose of laughter. In extremes, humor can be used to avoid dealing with difficulties or to avoid intimacy in relationships. On the other hand, humor is wonderful and therapeutic in a comfortable balance.

Don has a PhD, yet he can hardly read; he earned a good income, but now he cannot manage money; he used to give lectures, but now he cannot say what he means; he used to give counsel and now he gives answers that do not correlate with the questions. He can no longer do many of the things he found meaningful earlier in his life. So is there any hope in living this new way? Does he have any value to himself or to others? These are questions people often ask when life becomes difficult.

We believe that how we react to things makes more of a difference in our lives than what happens to us. How we do anything is more important than what we do. Our values, our character, our faith, our relationships, and how we treat people are all more significant than anything we can possess or accomplish.

Don says, "My life is still meaningful and good. It is very different from what I planned, but I choose to believe I still have meaning and value. Every day I try to improve someone's day. I try to find someone who looks dejected, and I try to cheer them up. I call people and ask them out for lunch because I think we both can benefit. I love people. I feel better about myself when I reach out to help someone else. I also read my Bible and pray more than when I was busy and working."

As a psychologist, Don encouraged many of his clients to read a book entitled *The Color of the Night*, by Gerhard E. Frost. The author drew profound insights on suffering from his reflections on the book of Job in the Bible. Although horrendous things happened, God held onto his servant Job with love that would not let go. Don and I have experienced peace from God through difficult times and a deep conviction that God loves us and will not abandon us.

Don and I have a good marriage; we have seen our sons grow up and marry wonderful women; we have become thrilled and proud grandparents; we have associated with wonderful people and have hundreds of friends; we have traveled the world. There are people who live in fear, hunger, and hatred, but that has not been our experience. We packed more into our first forty years than many people experience in a lifetime.

There are people who go through life with hardly a bump in the road, and yet they feel miserable and are miserable to be around. However, there are people who go through devastating tragedies and remain positive. We want to choose the latter.

Discouraging times could take Don into an emotional tailspin. When he nurses negative thoughts, he feels disheartened. If he feels down, he usually has to actively make a positive choice about what he thinks or does in order to escape a downward spiral. One trick he uses when he is alone and feeling down, is to watch *The Sound of Music*; he feels cheered up every time he watches that movie. When Don makes positive choices, he feels better about himself and life.

We have not solved all of our challenges since Don's stroke, but we continue to work on them and to learn. Interspersed between our difficulties are wonderful people and events that lift our spirits. There is still reason to look forward to meaningful life—still reason for hope.

Don chooses not to become bitter because he believes that God is loving and that He can bring good even out of difficulties in life. God is willing to listen when Don or I express our feelings of frustration and discouragement. We do not believe God caused this tragedy to punish Don. The stroke just happened. To grow angry and bitter would only hurt Don and strain his relationships with our family and friends.

Don's decision not to become bitter was difficult, and he occasionally needs to revisit his choice. However, his determination to be positive, instead of bitter, has affected the quality of our lives in such a positive way that we highly recommend it.

What helps us cope and gives us hope:

- We choose to value ourselves for who we are, rather than for our capabilities or possessions.
- We try to think of others and bring encouragement and cheer to them.
- We laugh.
- We have a good life. Even though we have come through difficult experiences, the good outweighs the bad.
- We are convinced that God loves us.

~

We did not choose Don's stroke,
but we can choose how we deal with it.

That gives us hope!

Organizations and Resources

The American Stroke Association,
   www.strokeassociation.org
National Stroke Association, www.stroke.org
   NSA's StrokeSmart™ Magazine
The Internet Stroke Center, www.strokecenter.org
Brain Injury Association of America, www.biausa.org
The DANA Foundation, www.Dana.org
The National Aphasia Association, www.aphasia.org
The Aphasia Hope Foundation, www.aphasiahope.org
Mayo Clinic, www.mayoclinic.org

Acknowledgments

Don would never be where he is without the countless people who came alongside to help him. We are grateful beyond words.

We thank the following dear family members and friends who encouraged us in Don's recovery. Some have also helped us make Don's dream of this book a reality: Josh and Beth Kvernen—our dear son and his wonderful wife, who love and support us and always make us proud; Svea Merry—our son Jon's wife, whom we love like a daughter, and who along with her second husband, Steve, and their combined children, bring great joy into our lives; Ruth Kvernen—Don's mother; Bev and Harold Nelson—Don's sister and her husband; Luther and Jan Kvernen—Don's brother and his wife; Lowie and Gene Sipprell—Don's sister and her husband; Marlene and Brad Walton—Rosella's sister and her husband; Kay Hawley—Don's reading tutor; Dorothy Peterson—Don's alternate reading tutor; Bob Sinex—Don's friend and catalyst for this book; Dick Tenley—Don's math practice friend; Marv Rylander—Don's reading practice friend; Staci Eischen—Don's physical therapist; Jarry and Linda Richardson—our friend, who is a psychiatrist, and his wife; Ken Wadum—Don's friend and former partner in his psychology practice; Mike and Sherrie Porterfield—people who became our dear friends when Mike was recovering from a brain tumor; Ann Peterson—Don's former boss at SEMCIL; and Joy Dekok, Joyce Washechek, and numerous other friends who helped improve our manuscript.

Glossary

ADA. *Americans with Disabilities Act.* Federal legislation enacted in 1990 to protect the rights of people with disabilities. The law promotes access and prohibits discrimination against those with disabilities. Don benefited from this legislation, which was passed shortly before his stroke.

AFO. Ankle-foot orthosis. This plastic brace extends from Don's toes to slightly under his knee and stabilizes his paralyzed foot. Without his AFO, he could not walk.

alexia. A condition in which a former reader acquires a reading disability. Don's stroke caused his alexia.

aneurysm. An abnormal weakening or bulging of a blood vessel, which can potentially rupture. Doctors continue to monitor Don's abdominal aortic aneurysm.

anomia. Difficulty with correctly naming people and things. Don has struggled with anomia.

anticoagulant. A medication that inhibits blood from clotting. Don took various anticoagulants, including heparin and warfarin (Coumadin) and for many years aspirin.

anticonvulsant. A medication used to treat seizure activity in the brain. Don had to try several different anticonvulsants before he found one that successfully treated his seizures without bothersome side effects.

aphasia. Partial or complete loss of the ability to communicate with written or spoken words. This can involve both expressive and receptive use of language. Don's aphasia has improved but still persists.

cognitive skills. Abilities to process thoughts, to perceive, reason, and learn. Although Don at times thinks clearly, his cognitive skills are often scrambled.

CPAP. *Continuous positive airway pressure.* A machine that consists of an air pump, tubing, and a face mask, used by people like Don who have obstructive sleep apnea. The CPAP has increased his quality of sleep and made him feel more rested during the day. He uses his CPAP at night and whenever he takes naps.

CT scan or CAT scan. *Computed tomograph.* A scan that employs a large series of cross-sectional x-rays to record images of the body. Don has had numerous CTs.

CVA. *Cerebrovascular accident.* Another term for stroke.

DVT. *Deep vein thrombosis.* A condition in which a clot forms in a deep vein, often in the leg. DVT is sometimes called the "economy class syndrome" because it can be precipitated by a long plane ride. Cramped conditions that limit movement, low cabin pressure, low humidity, and dehydration can all contribute to poor circulation and clot formation. There is a risk that the thrombus (clot) will dislodge and travel up the vein to a place where it will block blood flow. If the clot passes through the heart and blocks blood flow in the lungs, the condition is called a pulmonary embolism (PE) and can be fatal. In other cases a clot travels through the heart to the brain, resulting in a stroke (see PFO). This is one possible cause of Don's stroke.

dyslexia. A neurological difference that affects a person's ability to process language.

edema. Swelling from the accumulation of fluid in the body's tissue. In Don's case, his right arm and leg hang down with almost no muscle movement to help push his blood back up to his heart. Positioning the affected limb above his heart helps to relieve the edema, so when he gets up in the morning, his arm and lower leg are more normal in size. However, throughout the day, his edema increases considerably. Movement, wearing elastic stockings, and raising his legs in his recliner help minimize his edema.

epilepsy. A condition of recurrent seizures. Don's first seizure happened about nine months after his stroke. He experienced seizures about once a month until they were eventually controlled by anticonvulsants.

hemiplegia. Paralysis and loss of sensation on one side of the body, most often caused by stroke. Don has significant right-sided hemiplegia. (While damage inside the brain causes one-sided hemiplegia, spinal cord injury causes paraplegia, which is paralysis and loss of sensation on both sides of the body and affects anything controlled by nerves that leave the spinal cord below the injury. Hemiparesis is one-sided weakness.)

hemorrhagic stroke. A type of stroke that occurs when an artery leaks or ruptures and causes bleeding inside the brain. This was not Don's type of stroke.

ICU. *Intensive care unit.* A hospital unit that provides a more critical level of intensive medical care. Don spent six days in St. Marys Hospital's Neuro ICU.

internal carotid dissection. A tear of the internal carotid artery. On its way to the brain, blood flows up from the heart through the aorta to where it splits into the right and left common carotid arteries. These carotid arteries split into an internal and external branch. The tear and clot in Don's left internal carotid artery blocked the blood supply to roughly half of the left side of his brain.

ischemic stroke. A type of stroke caused by the blockage of an artery that supplies blood to the brain. In Don's case, a clot caused the ischemia.

kinesthetic learning. A learning style that uses touching and feeling or a physical activity in addition to listening, seeing, and hearing. This multisensory method was the key to Don's learning to read.

MRI. *Magnetic resonance imaging,* an imaging technique that uses magnets and radio waves to record images of the body (see Don's MRI in the photo section).

Orton-Gillingham Method. An approach to teaching reading, spelling, and writing that emphasizes kinesthetic learning. It is based on work done in the 1920s by Dr. Samuel Orton, then director of the Iowa State Psychopathic Hospital and professor of psychiatry at the University of Iowa. He went on to work at Columbia University. At his request, Miss Anna Gillingham, a psychologist and remedial teacher in New York, analyzed the structure of language and combined this with the teaching procedures he recommended. Don's tutor used this method with him.

perseveration. Uncontrolled repetition of a word(s) or activity.

Phlebotomy. Removal of venous blood, often for transfusion or diagnostic purposes. When Don developed an abnormally high red blood cell count due to inadequate CPAP pressure, his doctors prescribed phlebotomies, similar to the bloodletting of past centuries, for treatment.

PFO. *Patent foramen ovale.* Patent=open or unobstructed, foramen=a small opening or orifice, ovale=this particular opening. Before a baby is born, oxygen is drawn into a mother's blood through her lungs and delivered through the umbilical cord to the fetus. The little foramen ovale in the heart of the fetus allows blood to circulate without going through the lungs of the fetus. When a baby is born, its lungs take over and the little bypass hole closes. For some people the opening does not close. A PFO usually does not cause a problem. However, if an embolism arrives in the heart, the clot can slip through this opening and proceed to the brain, instead of the lungs. Don has a PFO that was not discovered until after he had his stroke.

PM&R. *Physical Medicine and Rehabilitation.* A branch of medicine that treats patients with physical impairments or disabilities.

pre-seizure aura. A warning sensation that some people experience before a seizure. Don's auras occurred one to two seconds before his seizures.

proprioception. An ability to sense the location or relative position of a body part. After Don's stroke, he could not tell where his right arm and leg were unless he looked.

prothrombin time. A diagnostic test that measures how long it takes for blood to coagulate or clot. When Don took anticoagulants, he had to have his prothrombin times checked frequently to help regulate the dosage.

psychologist. A trained and licensed mental health professional who provides psychological assessments and counseling or psychotherapy. Don was a psychologist.

psychiatrist. A physician (MD) who diagnoses and treats mental health disorders and is able to prescribe medications.

seizure. A temporary episode of brain malfunction with symptoms ranging from temporary mild loss of awareness to dramatic uncontrolled thrashing. There are a variety of types of seizures. A diagnosis of epilepsy means a patient has recurring seizures. Don had generalized seizures that lasted up to eight minutes.

SEMCIL. *Southeastern Minnesota Center for Independent Living.* Don participated in their support groups and worked for several years as a peer mentor for SEMCIL.

shoulder subluxation. A condition that can happen to stroke survivors when the upper arm is dislocated from the shoulder due to weakness in the shoulder muscles. Don's subluxation is not severe and does not cause pain.

sleep apnea. A condition in which breathing during sleep is dysfunctional, resulting in low levels of oxygen in the blood system. Before Don was treated for this with a CPAP machine, he snored loudly. His sleep was often interrupted when he snorted after short periods of not breathing.

SSDI. *Social Security Disability Income.* Federal benefits to those no longer able to work due to a permanent disability. We are grateful for the financial support we receive from SSDI.

stroke. A loss of brain function that occurs when an artery that supplies blood to the brain bursts or is blocked. Without oxygen-rich blood, the nerve cells in the affected area of the brain become damaged and begin to die. As a result, the parts of the body controlled by the damaged section of the brain can no longer function properly. (See also hemorrhagic stroke and ischemic stroke.)

TBI. *Traumatic brain injury.* An injury caused by accidental or violent force applied to the head that damages the brain.

TIA. *Transient ischemic attack.* Sometimes called ministrokes, TIAs are small episodes of interrupted blood flow to part of the brain. By definition, the condition and its symptoms resolve within minutes or hours. Don experienced two distinct TIAs the day before his stroke.

TouchMath. A multisensory program for teaching basic arithmetic skills, designed in 1975 by Janet Bullock, that has been expanded into a complete program used by many schools around the world.[1] It uses strategically placed TouchPoints on numerals that can be tapped with a pencil or finger as they are counted. The TouchPoints are used for teaching the meaning of the numeral and for basic computation. Don could not learn to read numbers before he tried this teaching method (see

---

1 Jane Bullock, B.S., M.A., Innovative Learning Concepts, 6760 Corporate Drive, Colorado Springs, Co. 80919-1999, 800-888-9191, info@touchmath.com, www.touchmath.com

TouchMath diagram in Chapter 6).

tPA. *Tissue plasminogen activator*. A clot-busting drug. In recent years (after Don's stroke) advances in early treatment with tPA have reduced the early damage of stroke and improved the chances of greater recovery.

TGA. *Transient global amnesia*. A medical condition in which a person temporarily loses short-term memory. Don had a handful of episodes of TGA a few years ago.

waiver of premium. A clause in an insurance policy that allows coverage to continue without the policyholder's payment of premiums. We benefited from this feature on some of our policies, but we had a problem with another policy.

About the Authors

Don Kvernen qualifies by personal experience to speak about stroke recovery. At the age of forty, his doctors diagnosed him as "completely and permanently disabled" by a stroke. Although he can no longer work as a psychologist, he regularly visits other men who have experienced stroke or traumatic brain injury to encourage and befriend them. With his positive attitude, Don makes friends wherever he goes. He is also a determined individual. Even though many losses from his stroke are permanent, he has made remarkable recovery and adjustments.

Don grew up on a farm in eastern North Dakota. He began his education in a country school and earned a bachelor's degree in Social Science and Education from North Dakota State University. After college, he worked with youth in northwestern Wisconsin and with youth in a boarding school for missionary kids in Pakistan. Don earned a master's degree and a doctorate in Counseling and Guidance from the University of North Dakota. For eight-and-a-half years before his stroke, he worked as a licensed consulting psychologist in his private counseling practice in Rochester, Minnesota, and provided consulting and counseling for international missionaries. He has participated in FarmHouse Fraternity, Blue Key Honor Society, InterVarsity

Christian Fellowship, NDSU Concert Choir, Rotary, and his local church.

Don's wife, Rosella, shares her experience as a wife and care partner. She grew up in western Minnesota. Rosella earned diplomas from the California Lutheran Bible School in Los Angeles, California, and from St. Luke's Hospital School of Nursing in Fargo, North Dakota. She left nursing to raise their two sons. For many years, she volunteered for her children's activities and at her church. She enjoys playing piano and cello, inventing, fixing things, gardening, creating spreadsheets, making international friends, and talking with strangers.

Don and Rosella Kvernen speak openly and positively despite the adversities they have experienced with Don's disabling stroke and the more recent death of their older son from cancer. They exemplify the fact that *there IS life after stroke*. Even though Don's stroke sent ripples into every area of their lives, they believe that how they react to whatever life brings is more significant than what happens to them. Their daily goal is to be a positive influence in the lives of people around them.